PIANO / VOCAL / GUITAR

THE BEST MOVIE SOUNDTRACK SONGS EVER

ISBN 978-1-4950-2264-7

HAL•LEONARD®
CORPORATION
7777 W. BLUEMOUND RD. P.O. BOX 13819 MILWAUKEE, WI 53213

Visit Hal Leonard Online at
www.halleonard.com

AGAINST ALL ODDS
(Take a Look at Me Now)
from AGAINST ALL ODDS

Words and Music by
PHIL COLLINS

Moderately slow

Dm7 Gsus G Dm7 G
mf
A7sus Am7 Bm7 C(add2) Dm7(add4) Dm7
How can I just let you walk a - way, just let you leave with - out a trace, when I
F(add2) F G/F Em7 Am
stand here tak - ing ev - 'ry breath with you? Ooh. You're the

** Recorded a half step lower.*

Dm7
G
on - ly one who real - ly knew me at all.
A7sus
Am7
Bm7
C(add2)
Dm7(add4)
3fr
Dm7
How can you just walk a - way from me, when all I can do is watch you leave? 'Cause we've
wish I could just make you turn a - round, turn a - round and see me cry. There's so
F(add2)
F
G/F
Em7
Am
shared the laugh - ter and the pain, and e - ven shared the tears.
much I need to say to you, so man - y rea - sons why.
You're the

Dm7
Gsus
3fr
G
only one who really knew me at all.
So take a look at me now,
C/G
D7/G
well, there's just an empty space,
and there's nothing
3
3
Am7
F
Dm7
Gsus
3fr
left here to remind me, just a mem - 'ry of your face.
{Ooh, Now,}
take a look at me now,

C/G
D7/G
well, there's just an emp-ty space, and you com-ing back
'cause but to wait
Am7
F
1 Dm7
Gsus
3fr
to me is a - gainst the odds, and that's what I've got to face.
for you is all I can do, and that's what
G
2 Dm7
Gsus
3fr
G
I I've got to face. Take a good look at me now,

C/G
D7/G
'cause I'll still be stand-ing here, and you com-ing back
Am7
F
Dm7
to me is a - gainst all odds, it's the chance I've got - ta take.
Gsus
3fr
G
Dm7
Gsus
G
Dm7
G
Dm7
Csus2
Gsus2/B
F(add2)
G
Take a look at me now.
rit.

BECAUSE YOU LOVED ME

from UP CLOSE AND PERSONAL

Words and Music by
DIANE WARREN

Slowly
D
For all those times you stood by me, for all the
wings and made me fly. You touched my
mf
G
truth that you made me see, for all the
hand, I could touch the sky. I lost my
Bm7
joy you brought to my life, for all the
faith, you gave it back to me. You said no
Asus
wrong that you made right, for ev - 'ry
star was out of reach. You stood by
F♯m7
dream you made come true, for all the
me and I stood tall. I had your

* *Recorded a half step lower.*

Gmaj7
Em7/A
love I found in you, I'll be for - ev - er thank - ful, ba - by.
love, I had it all. I'm grate - ful for each day you gave me.
C6
Bm7
Em7
You're the one who held me up, nev - er let me fall.
May - be I don't know that much, but I know this much is true:
Gm7
Em7/A
You're the one who saw me through, through it all.
I was blessed be - cause I was loved by you.
You were my
D
G
strength when I was weak. You were my voice when I could-n't speak. You were my

Bm7
Asus
A
eyes when I could-n't see. You saw the best there was in me, lift-ed me
F♯m7
Gmaj9
Cmaj7
up when I could-n't reach. You gave me faith 'cause you be-lieved. I'm
Em7/A
To Coda
1
D
Em7/A
ev-'ry-thing I am be-cause you loved me. You gave me
2
D
F♯7/A♯
4fr
Bm7
loved me. You were al-ways there for me, the ten-der wind that car-ried me, a

F#7/A#
Bm7
light in the dark, shin-ing your love in-to my life. You've
Em7
D/F#
been my in-spi-ra-tion. Through the lies you were the truth. My
Em7/A
D.S. al Coda
world is a bet-ter place be-cause of you. You were my
CODA
D
F#m7/B
E
loved me. Bkgd. Vocal: (You were my strength when I was weak. You were my
Lead vocal ad lib.

A
C♯m7
4fr
voice when I could-n't speak. You were my eyes when I could-n't see. You saw the
Bsus
G♯m7
4fr
best there was in me, lift-ed me up when I could-n't reach. You gave me
Amaj9
Dmaj7
F♯m7/B
faith 'cause you be-lieved.) Lead vocal: I'm ev-'ry-thing I am be-cause you
E
F♯m7/B
E
loved me. I'm ev-'ry-thing I am be-cause you loved me.

AMERICA

from the Motion Picture THE JAZZ SINGER

Words and Music by
NEIL DIAMOND

Moderately bright
F
mf
Far, we've been trav - el - ing far,
with - out a home,
but not with-out a star.

Free, on - ly want to be free.
We hud - dle close, hang on to a dream.
G
On the boats and on the planes,
they're com - ing to A - mer - i - ca.

Nev - er look - ing back ___ a - gain, they're com - ing to A -
D/F♯
Em
D
mer - i - ca. Home, don't it seem so
G
C/E
G
D
far a - way. Oh, we're trav - el - ing light to - day,
Em
F
G/D
F/E♭
in the eye of the storm, ___ in the eye of the

Em
storm.
Home
D
G
to a new and a shin - y place.
C/E
G
Make our bed, and we'll say
D
our grace,
Em
F
free-dom's light burn - ing warm,
G/D
F/E♭
Em
free-dom's light burn - ing warm.

F
Ev - 'ry - where a - round the world,
they're com - ing to A - mer - i - ca.
Ev - 'ry time that flag's
un - furled,
they're com - ing to A - mer - i - ca.

G
Got a dream to take them there.
They're com - ing to A - mer - i - ca.
Got a dream, they've come to share.
They're com - ing to A - mer - i - ca.
A
They're com - ing to A - mer - i - ca.
F♯m7
They're com - ing to A - mer - i - ca.

D
Bm7
They're com - ing to A - mer - i - ca. They're com - ing to A -
A
mer - i - ca to - day, to - day,
F♯m7
D
to - day,
Bm7
to - day, to - day.

A
F♯m
My coun - try 'tis of thee (to - day), sweet land of
D
lib - er - ty (to - day), of thee I sing (to - day),
Bm
F
of thee I sing to - day.
Repeat and Fade
To - day, to - day.

ARTHUR'S THEME
(Best That You Can Do)
from ARTHUR an ORION PICTURES release through WARNER BROS.

Words and Music by BURT BACHARACH,
CAROLE BAYER SAGER, CHRISTOPHER CROSS
and PETER ALLEN

Moderately
Dm7
G7
C
mf
F
B♭
E7
A
E/A
A
A/C♯
Dm7
Once in your life, you'll find
Ar - thur, he does what he
G7
C
F
her, some - one who turns your heart a - round, and
pleas - es. All of his life, his mas - ter's toys, and

B♭
E7sus
E7
A
next thing you know, you're clos - in' down the town.
deep in his heart, he's just, he's just a boy.
E/A
A
A/C♯
Dm7
Wake up and she's still with
Liv - in' his life one day
G7
C
you, e - ven though you left her way
at a time, he's show - ing him - self a real -
F
B♭
a - cross town. You're won - der - in' to your -
ly good time. He's laugh - in' a - bout the

E7sus
E7
A
E/A
A
A/C♯
self, hey, what-'ve I found?
way they want him to be.
Dmaj7
E/D
D
When you get caught be-tween the moon and New York
Amaj7
Bm7
A/B
Cit-y, I know it's cra-zy,
Bm7
A
A/C♯
but it's true.

Dmaj7
E/D
D
C♯m7
If you get caught be - tween the moon and New York Cit -
F♯7sus
F♯7
Bm7
y, the best that you can do, the
D/A
best that you can do is fall in love.
1
A
A/C♯
2
D.S. and Fade
A
A/C♯
Optional Ending
A

BEAUTY AND THE BEAST

from Walt Disney's BEAUTY AND THE BEAST

Music by ALAN MENKEN
Lyrics by HOWARD ASHMAN

Eb(add9) Eb Bb7sus Bb7 Eb(add9) Eb
3fr
Just a lit - tle change. Small, to say the
Bbm7 Eb7 Abmaj7 Gm7 Fm7 Bb7sus Bb7
least. Both a lit - tle scared, nei - ther one pre - pared. Beau - ty and the
poco rit.
Eb(add9) Bb7sus Gm
Beast. Ev - er just the same.
a tempo
mf
Ab(add9) Ab Gm Ab(add9) Ab
4fr
Ev - er a sur - prise. Ev - er as be -

Gm7
Cm
Cm7
D♭
E♭
fore, ev - er just as sure as the sun will rise.
F
C7sus
C7
F(add9)
F
Tale as old as time.
Tune as old as
C7sus
C7
F(add9)
F
Am
song.
Bit - ter - sweet and strange, find - ing you can
B♭(add9)
B♭
B♭/C
C7
F(add9)
F
C7sus
change, learn - ing you were wrong.
Cer - tain as the sun
f

F(add9) F Cm F7 B♭maj7 Am7
ris - ing in the East. Tale as old as time, song as old as
Gm7 F/C C7 F(add9) F/E Dm Am/C B♭ Am
rhyme. Beau-ty and the Beast. Tale as old as time, song as old as
poco rit.
dim.
slower
Gm7 C7sus C7 F(add9) Fsus F(add9)
rhyme. Beau-ty and the Beast.
a tempo
Fsus F
8va
rit.

BELIEVE

from Warner Bros. Pictures' THE POLAR EXPRESS

Words and Music by GLEN BALLARD
and ALAN SILVESTRI

Moderately slow
E
G♯m/D♯
mp
With pedal
Chil - dren sleep - ing, snow is soft - ly
Trains move quick - ly to their jour - ney's
fall - ing.
end.
F♯m
E♭
Dreams are call - ing
Des - ti - na - tions
A
B
like bells in the dis - tance.
are where we be - gin a - gain.

E
G♯m/D♯
4fr
E
We were dream - ers, not so long a - go,
Ships go sail - ing far a - cross the sea,
G♯m/D♯
4fr
F♯m
E♭
3fr
but one by one, we
trust - ing star - light
F♯m
A
B
to all had to grow up.
to get where they need to be.
G♯m
4fr
A
When it seems the mag - ic slipped a - way, we
When it seems that we have lost our way, we
mf

D/F♯
1
To next strain
Bsus
B
find it all a - gain on Christ - mas Day. Be -
find our - selves a - gain on Christ - mas
2
Bsus
B
Day. Be -
cresc.
E
F♯m11
lieve in what your heart is say - ing,
E9/G♯
A
E
B(add4)/D♯
hear the mel - o - dy that's play - ing. There's no time to waste, there's so
F♯m7
E/B
Bsus
E
F♯m11
much to cel - e - brate. Be - lieve in what you feel in - side and

E9/G♯
6fr
G♯7♯5
4fr
C♯m
4fr
give your dreams the wings _ to fly.
F♯m7
B7sus
2fr
You have ev - 'ry - thing you _ need _ if you just _
1
E
G♯m/D♯
4fr
_ be - lieve.
8va
2
E
F♯m11
_ be - lieve.
E9/G♯
6fr
A
E
B(add4)/D♯
4fr
F♯m7
E/B
Bsus
If you just _ be - lieve, if you just _

E
F♯m11
E9/G♯
6fr
A
E
B(add4)/D♯
4fr
be - lieve.
If you just
be - lieve.
F♯m7
E/B
Bsus
E
F♯m11
E9/G♯
6fr
A
Just be - lieve,
just
E
B(add4)/D♯
4fr
F♯m7
E/B
Bsus
E
F♯m11
be - lieve.
Repeat and Fade
Optional Ending
E9/G♯
6fr
A
E
B(add4)/D♯
4fr
F♯m7
E/B
Bsus
E

CHARIOTS OF FIRE

from CHARIOTS OF FIRE

By VANGELIS

D♭ G♭/D♭ D♭ G♭/D♭ D♭ G♭/D♭
D♭ G♭/D♭ D♭ G♭/D♭ D♭ G♭/D♭ D♭ G♭/A♭
D♭ Fm G♭ D♭ Fm A♭7 D♭
Fm G♭ D♭ G♭/A♭ D♭ Fm G♭ D♭
Fm A♭7 D♭
1
Fm G♭ D♭ G♭/A♭ D♭ G♭/D♭

2
Fm
Gb
Db
Ab7
Db
Gb/Db
Db
Gb/Db
Db
Gb/Db
Db
Gb/Db
Db
Gb/Db
Db
Gb/Db
Db
Gb/Db
Db
Gb/Db
Db
Gb/Db
Db
Gb/Db
Db
Gb/Db
Db
Gb/Db
Db

CHARADE

from CHARADE

Music by HENRY MANCINI
Words by JOHNNY MERCER

F/A
Am6
F/A
Oh, what a hit we made,
Am
Bm7(no5)
E7
we came on next to clos - ing.
Bm7(no5)
E7
Bm7(no5)
E7
Best on the bill, lov - ers un - til
Bm7(no5)
E+
E7
Am
love left the mas - que - rade.

Dm7
G9
9fr
Cmaj7
Am
Fate seemed to pull the strings. I
Dm
G7
C
C♯dim
4fr
turned and you were gone,
Dm7
G7
Cmaj7
Am
while from the dark - ened wings the
D9
4fr
Bm7(no5)
E7
mu - sic box played on.

Am
Sad lit - tle ser - e - nade,
song of my
E7
Bm7(no5)
E7
heart's com - pos - ing.
I hear it still,
Bm7(no5)
E7
Bm7♭5
E7♯5(♭9)
6fr
I al - ways will,
best on the bill
rit.
E7
Am
Am6
cha - rade.
a tempo

CIRCLE OF LIFE

from Walt Disney Pictures' THE LION KING

Music by ELTON JOHN
Lyrics by TIM RICE

Relaxed Pop beat

B♭
Cm/B♭
8fr
day we ar - rive on the plan - et and
Some of us fall by the way - side, and
F7/A
3fr
B♭
F/A
blink - ing, step in - to the sun, there's
some of us soar to the stars. And
Gm
3fr
Cm
3fr
more to be seen than can ev - er be seen, more to do
some of us sail through our trou - bles, and some
A♭
4fr
F
F7/A
3fr
than can ev - er be done.
have to live with the scars. There's

B♭
Cm/B♭
8fr
Some say, "Eat or be eat - en." Some say,
far too much to take in here, more to
F7/A
3fr
B♭
F/A
"Live and let live." But
find than can ev - er be found. But the
Gm7
Cm
3fr
all are a - greed as they join the stam - pede, you should
sun roll - ing high through the sap - phi - re sky keeps great and
cresc.
A♭
4fr
F
nev - er take more than you give in the cir - cle of life.
small on the end - less round in the cir - cle of life.

Bb
Eb/Bb
Bb
It's the wheel of for -
f
Ab/Bb
- tune.
It's the leap of faith.
Eb
Ab/Eb
Eb
It's the band of hope
F/Eb
'til we find our place

B♭/D
G7
Cm
on the path un-wind - ing
G♭(add2)
B♭/F
To Coda
in the cir - cle,
1
F
E♭/B♭
B♭
the cir - cle of life.
dim.
2
F
B♭
D.S. al Coda
E♭/B♭
the cir - cle of life!

CODA
F
E♭/B♭
the cir - cle of life.
dim.
B♭
Cm/B♭
B♭
G/B
On the path un - wind -
mp
Cm
G♭(add2)
B♭/F
- ing
in the cir - cle,
F
E♭/B♭
G♭/B♭
B♭
the cir - cle of life.
rall.

COME WHAT MAY

from the Motion Picture MOULIN ROUGE

Words and Music by
DAVID BAERWALD

Slowly
C
D7
Fsus2
mf
D7
Fsus2
Fmaj7
C
D7sus
D7
Fsus2
Male: Nev - er knew I could feel like this,
like I've nev - er seen the sky

C G/B Am7 C/D D7
be - fore. Want to van - ish in - side your kiss.
Fsus2 C G/B
Ev - 'ry day I love you more and more.
Am7 D7sus D7
Lis - ten to my heart. Can you hear it sing and
G9sus G Csus C G/B Am C/G
tell - ing me to give you ev - 'ry - thing? Sea - sons may change,

D
C/G
win - ter to spring,
but I love you un - til the
Fmaj7/G
G
C
G/B
Am
end of time. Come what may,
come what may,
D7
I will
C
C/G
G
G7
C
love you un - til my dy - ing day.

D7sus
D7
Female: Sud-den-ly the world seems such a per - fect place.
Fsus2
C
G/B
Sud - den - ly it moves with such a per - fect grace.
Am
D7sus
D7
Both: Sud - den - ly my life does - n't seem such a waste.
Fsus2
C
G/B
Female: It all re - volves a - round you.
Both: And there's no moun -

Am
C/D
D
- tain too high, no riv - er too wide.
Gsus
G
Csus
C
G/B
Am
Am/G
Sing out this song, and I'll be there by your side.
Storm clouds may gath - er and
D/F♯
D
C/G
stars may col - lide,
Female: I love you
Male: but I love you un - til the
Fmaj7/G
G
C
G/B
Am
un - til the end of time.
end of time.
Both: Come what may,

G/A Am D7sus D7
come what may, I will
C C/G G7 C Em/B
love you un - til my dy - ing day. Oh, come what
Am Cmaj7/D D7
3fr
may, come what may,
D7sus D7 Csus Em/B Em Fmaj7
I will love you.
I will love, I will love you.

Dm7 Em7 F Ab Bb
Female: Sud-den-ly the world seems such a per - fect place.
C F/C C
Both: Come what may, come what
F/C Am C/G F
may, I will love _ you _ un - til my
C/G G7 C
dy - ing _ day.
rall.

CUPS
(When I'm Gone)
from the Motion Picture Soundtrack PITCH PERFECT

Words and Music by A.P. CARTER,
LUISA GERSTEIN and HELOISE TUNSTALL-BEHRENS

Moderate Folk
C
mp
I got my tick-et for the
F
C
long way 'round,
two bot-tle o' whis-key for the
way.
And I
Am
G
F
Dm
G
sure would like some
sweet com-pa-ny.
And I'm
leav-in' to-mor-row, what do ya

C
Am
F
say? When I'm gone, when I'm gone,
Am
G
you're gon - na miss me when I'm gone.
You're gon - na
You're gon - na
Am
G
F
miss me by my hair, you'll miss me ev - 'ry - where. Oh,
miss me by my walk, you're gon - na miss me by my talk. Oh,
Dm
G
C
you're gon - na miss me when I'm gone. When I'm
you're gon - na miss me when I'm gone. When I'm

Am
F
Am
gone, when I'm gone, you're gon - na miss me when I'm
gone, when I'm gone, you're gon - na miss me when I'm
G
Am
G
gone. You're gon - na miss me by my walk, you're gon - na
gone. You're gon - na miss me by my hair, you're gon - na
F
Dm
G
To Coda
miss me by my talk. Oh, you're gon - na miss me when I'm
miss me ev - 'ry - where. Oh, you're sure gon - na miss me when I'm
C
gone.

I got my tick - et for the
F
C
long way 'round, the one with the pret - ti - est of views. It's got
Am
G
F
moun - tains, it's got riv - ers, it's got sights to give you shiv - ers, but it
Dm
G7
C
D.S. al Coda
sure would be pret - ti - er with you. When I'm

CODA
C
Am
gone. When I'm gone, when I'm
F
Am
gone, you're gon - na miss me when I'm
G
Am
G
gone. You're gon - na miss me by my walk, you're gon - na
F
Fm
Dm
G
C
miss me by my talk. Oh, you're gon - na miss me when I'm gone.

DAYS OF WINE AND ROSES

from DAYS OF WINE AND ROSES

Lyric by JOHNNY MERCER
Music by HENRY MANCINI

Moderately
F
F
Cm6/E♭
D7♭5(♭9)
D9
4fr
4fr
The days of wine and ros - es
mf
Gm
3fr
B♭m
laugh and run a - way like a child at play, through the
Am
Dm
Gm
3fr
Gm7
Em7♭5
A9
5fr
mead - ow - land to - ward a clos - ing door, a door marked "Nev - er - more," that

Dm7♭5 G9 Gm7 C7 F Cm6/E♭
9fr
wasn't there before. The lonely night dis-
D7♭5(♭9) D9 Gm B♭m
4fr 4fr 3fr
closes just a passing breeze filled with memories
Am Dm Dm7/C Bm7♭5 B♭9 Am Dm
of the golden smile that introduced me to the days of wine and
Gm9 Gm7/C F Fdim Gm7 C7 F C7/F Fmaj9
1 2
3fr 8fr
roses and you. The you.
rall.

DO YOU KNOW WHERE YOU'RE GOING TO?

Theme from MAHOGANY

Words by GERRY GOFFIN
Music by MICHAEL MASSER

Moderately, with expression
G♭
C♭
A♭m
B♭7
3
4fr
mf
E♭m
6fr
E♭m/G♭
3fr
A♭m6/C♭
B♭7
E♭
3fr
A♭
4fr
Fm
G7
Do you know where you're go - ing to?
Do you like the things that life is
Cm
3fr
Cm/E♭
3fr
Fm6/A♭
6fr
G7
C
show - ing you? Where are you go - ing to,
do you know?

Eb Ab Fm G7
Do you get what you're hop - ing for? When you look be - hind you there's no
Cm Cm/Eb Fm6/Ab G7
To Coda
o - pen door. What are you hop - ing for, do you
C D/C G/B G A
know? Once we were stand - ing still in time,
Dm7 F/G G7 C F/C C
chas - ing the fan - ta - sies that filled our minds. And you knew

D/C
Bm7
Em7
how I loved you but my spir - it was free,
Am7
C/D
D7
G7sus
G7
laugh-ing at the ques - tions that you once asked of me.
E♭
A♭
3fr
4fr
Fm
G7
Do you know where you're go - ing to? Do you like the things that life is
Cm
Cm/E♭
Fm6/A♭
G7
C
3fr
3fr
6fr
show - ing you? Where are you go - ing to, do you know?

E♭ A♭ Fm G7
mp
Cm Cm/E♭ Fm6/A♭ G7
C D/C G/B G A
Now looking back at all we planned,
f
Dm7 F/G G7 C F/C C
we let so many dreams just slip through our hands.

D/C
Bm7
Em7
Why must we wait so long before we see
Am7
C/D
D7
G7sus
G7
D.S. al Coda
how sad the an - swers to those ques - tions can be?
CODA
C
F
Dm
E7
know?
3
Am
Am/C
Dm6/F
E7

A
D
Bm
C♯7
3
F♯m
F♯m/A
Bm6/D
C♯7
G♭
C♭
A♭m
4fr
B♭7
3
E♭m
6fr
E♭m/G♭
3fr
A♭m6/C♭
B♭7
E♭
3fr

ENDLESS LOVE

from ENDLESS LOVE

Words and Music by
LIONEL RICHIE

E♭/F
Fsus
F
B♭
F/A
you're ev - 'ry step I make.
I can't re - sist your charms.
And
And
E♭maj7
E♭/F
F
B♭
F/A
3fr
I, I want to share all my
love, I'll be a fool for
mf
Gm
Dm/F
E♭
E♭/F
F
love with you; no one else
you, I'm sure; you know I don't
B♭
B♭9
E♭maj7
will do. And your eyes,
mind. 'Cause you,

Eb/F
F
Bb
F/A
Gm
F6
3fr
they tell me how much you care. Oh,
you mean the world to me. Oh,
Eb
Dm7
Cm7
3fr
yes, you will al - ways be
I know I've found in you
Eb/F
1
Bb
my end - less love.
my end - less
8va
mp
2
Bb
love.
mp

Eb
3fr
Eb/F
Fsus
F
Bb
Eb
3fr
Eb/F
Bb
Eb
3fr
Oh, and love,
cresc.
mf

E♭/F F B♭ F/A Gm7 F
I'll be that fool for you, I'm
E♭ E♭/F F B♭
sure; you know I don't mind.
B♭9 E♭ E♭/F F
And yes, you'll be the
B♭ F/A Gm Dm/F E♭maj7
on - ly one. No one can de - ny

Dm7
E♭maj7
3fr
Dm7
this love I have in - side. I'll
E♭maj7
3fr
Dm7
Cm7
3fr
give it all to you, my love, my love,
E♭/F
B♭
3
my end - less love.
3
p
3
3
E♭
3fr
E♭/F
Fsus
F
E♭/B♭
6fr
B♭
L.H.
rit.

EYE OF THE TIGER

Theme from ROCKY III

Words and Music by FRANK SULLIVAN
and JIM PETERIK

Cm
3fr
A♭/C
3fr
So man - y times it hap - pens too fast.
Face to face, out in the heat,
Ris - in' up, straight to the top.
B♭/C
Cm
3fr
You trade your pas - sion for glo - ry.
hang - in' tough, stay - in' hun - gry.
Had the guts, got the glo - ry.
Don't lose your grip on the
They stack the odds, still we
Went the dis - tance. Now I'm
A♭/C
3fr
3
B♭/C
dreams of the past. You must fight just to keep them a - live.
take to the street for the kill with the skill to sur - vive.
not gon - na stop, just a man and his will to sur - vive.

Cm
B♭
Cm7
Fm
E♭/G
B♭
Cm7
It's the eye of the ti - ger. It's the thrill of the fight, ris - in'
Fm
Cm7
B♭
Cm7
Fm
up to the chal-lenge of our ri - val. And the last known sur-vi - vor stalks his
E♭/G
B♭
Cm7
Fm
E♭/G
1, 2
A♭
N.C.
prey in the night, and he's watch - in' us all with the eye of the ti -
Cm
3
A♭
- ger.
eye

Cm
N.C.
of the ti - ger.
Cm7 B♭/C Cm7
B♭/C Cm7
Cm A♭/C
Cm
Cm7 B♭/C Cm7
B♭/C Cm7
The eye of the ti - ger.
Cm A♭/C
Repeat and Fade
Optional Ending
Cm C5 B♭5 C5
The eye of the ti - ger.

FALLING SLOWLY

from the Motion Picture ONCE

Words and Music by GLEN HANSARD
and MARKETA IRGLOVA

Am7
G
Fsus2
G
Am7
G
Games that nev - er a - mount to more than they're meant will play them-selves
F9
Fsus2
C
out. Take this sink - in'
Fsus2
Am7
Fsus2
boat and point it home; we've still got time.
C
Fsus2
Am7
Raise your hope - ful voice; you have a choice; you make it

Fsus2
C
now.
Fall - ing slow - ly,
decresc.
mp
Fsus2
C
Fsus2
eyes that know me and I can't go back.
And
C
Fsus2
C
moods that take me and e - rase me, and I'm paint - ed black.
Fsus2
Am
Em/G
Fsus2
G
Well, you have suf-fered e - nough and warred with your -

Am G6 Fsus2
self; it's time that you won.
cresc.
C Fsus2 Am7
Take this sink - in' boat and point it home; we've still got
mf
Fsus2 C Fsus2
time. Raise your hope - ful voice; you have a
Am7 Fsus2 C
choice; you've made it now. Fall - in' slow - ly,

Fsus2
Am7
Fsus2
sing your mel - o - dy; I'll sing it loud.
C
Fsus2
Am7
(Strings)
Fsus2
G/F
8va
Take it all.
Fsus2
I paid the cost too late,

G/F
now you're gone.
Fmaj9
Fsus2
C
Fsus2
C
Fsus2
C
rit.

FLASHDANCE...WHAT A FEELING

from the Paramount Picture FLASHDANCE

Lyrics by KEITH FORSEY and IRENE CARA
Music by GIORGIO MORODER

Steadily
B♭ F Cm Gm
mf
B♭ F Cm
First, when there's noth - ing but a slow glow - ing
Gm E♭ B♭
dream that your fear seems to hide deep in -
A♭ E♭/F F B♭
side your mind, all a - lone I have
3fr
4fr
3

F
Cm
3fr
Gm
3fr
cried si - lent tears full of pride in a
Faster, with a driving beat
E♭
3fr
B♭
A♭
4fr
E♭
3fr
world made of steel, made of stone.
f
A♭
4fr
E♭/F
F
E♭/F
F
Well,
B♭
F
Cm
3fr
I hear the mu - sic, close my eyes, feel the
I hear the mu - sic, close my eyes, I am

Gm Eb Bb
rhy - thm wrap a - round, take a hold of my
rhy - thm. In a flash it takes hold of my
Ab Eb/F F Gm F
heart.
heart.
What a feel - ing,
Eb F Gm F Eb F
be - in's be - liev - in'. I can have
Bb Cm7 F7 Bb/D Eb Eb/F F7
it all. Now I'm danc - ing for my life.

E♭/F F7 Gm F E♭ F
Take your pas - sion and make it hap -
Gm F E♭ F B♭ Cm7 F7
- pen. Pic-tures come a - live. You can dance
Now I'm danc -
To Coda
B♭/D E♭ E♭/F F7 F
right through your life.
- ing through my life.
3
B♭ F B♭ Cm Gm

E♭
3fr
B♭
A♭
4fr
E♭/F
F7
D.S. al Coda
3
Now
3
CODA
E♭/F
F7
E♭/F
F7
What a feel-
A♭
4fr
G♭
A♭
4fr
G♭
A♭
4fr
F7
- ing.
E♭
3fr
F
E♭
3fr
F
A♭
4fr
G♭
A♭
4fr
G♭
A♭
4fr

F7 Eb F Gm F
What a feel - ing,
(I am
Eb F Gm F Eb F
be - in's be - liev - in'. Pic - tures come
mu - sic now.) (I am rhy - thm now.)
Bb Cm7 Bb/D Eb Eb/F
a - live, you can dance right through your life.
Repeat and Fade
Optional Ending
F Gm F Eb F Gm
What a feel - ing. What a feel - ing.
(I can real - ly have it all.)

FOOTLOOSE

Theme from the Paramount Picture FOOTLOOSE

Words by DEAN PITCHFORD
Music by KENNY LOGGINS

A
D/A
A
I been work - in' so hard. I'm punch - in'
You're play - in' so cool, o - bey - ing
D/A
A
D/A
my card. Eight hours, for what?
ev - 'ry rule. Dig way down in your heart
A
D
Oh, tell me what I got. I've got this
you're burn - in', yearn - in' for some, some - bod - y to
feel - in' that time's just hold - in' me down.
tell you that life ain't pass - in' you by.

Omit 2nd time
A
D
I'll hit the ceil - in',
I'm try - in' to tell you
D♯dim
6fr
B7
E
or else I'll tear up this town.
it will if you don't e - ven fly.
F♯m7
Gdim7
E/G♯
N.C.
To-night I got - ta cut
You can fly if you'd on - ly cut

A D/A A D
(1.,3.) loose, foot - loose; kick off your Sun - day
(2.) loose, foot - loose; kick off your Sun - day
A D/A A
shoes. Please, Lou - ise,
shoes. Ooh - ee, Ma - rie,
D A D/A
pull me off of my knees. Jack, get
shake it, shake it for me. Whoa, Mi -
A D A
back; come on be - fore we crack.
lo, come on, come on let's go.

To Coda
D/A
A
G
D
Lose your blues, ev - 'ry - bod - y cut foot -
Lose your blues,
A
loose.
G
D
A
N.C.
ev - 'ry - bod - y cut foot - loose.
Cut foot - loose.
Cut foot - loose.

A5
5fr
N.C.
First, you've got to turn me a - round,
A5
5fr
N.C.
sec - ond, and put your feet
on the ground.
A5
5fr
N.C.
Third, now, take a hold of your soul.
E7♯9
6fr
N.C.
D.S. al Coda
I'm turn - in' it

CODA
N.C.
G D/F♯
N.C.
ev - 'ry - bod - y cut, ev - 'ry - bod - y cut, ev - 'ry - bod - y cut, ev - 'ry -
G D/F♯
N.C.
D
N.C.
bod - y cut, ev - 'ry - bod - y cut, ev - 'ry - bod - y cut, ev - 'ry - bod - y,
A
ev - 'ry - bod - y cut foot - loose.

GONNA FLY NOW

Theme from ROCKY

By BILL CONTI,
AYN ROBBINS and CAROL CONNORS

Dm7
Cmaj7
read - y to make a move, yeah.
Rocky's / Now I'm
Dm7
Cmaj7
Dm7
Em7
read - y he / I just can't lose, yeah.
Ev-'ry nerve a wire
Fmaj7
Esus
sweat - in' blood, like fire.
Dm7
Cmaj7
Bod-y's ach - in' from the hurt it's tak - in', mus-cles

Dm7
Cmaj7
Dm7
Em7
scream - in' like a burn - in' de - mon.
Ev - 'ry nerve a wire
Fmaj7
Esus
sweat - in' blood, like fire.
Dm7
Try - in' hard now,
Feel - in' strong now,
Em7
Fmaj7
B♭maj7
it's so hard now,
won't be long now,

Asus
Dm7
try - in' hard now, Rock - y pow - er by the
get - tin' strong now, fists like thun - der gon - na put you
Cmaj7
Dm7
Cmaj7
hour, pump - in' i - ron God ya know he's try - in'.
un - der, pump - in' i - ron God ya know I'm try - in'.
Dm7
Em7
Fmaj7
Ev - 'ry nerve a wire sweat - in' blood, like
Esus
fire. Gon - na

Dm7/G
Cmaj7/G
fly now, fly - ing high now.
Fmaj7
Dm7
Bm7♭5
Gon-na fly, fly,
1
Esus
2
Esus
fly. fly.
Am

FORTY-SECOND STREET

from 42ND STREET

Words by AL DUBIN
Music by HARRY WARREN

Dm G7 Cmaj7 C Em Em(maj7)
"Wall Street Jack" built, if you've got a lit - tle
Em7 Em6 Em C6 C7 B7
time to spare, I want to take you there.
poco rit.
Em B7 Em B7
Come and meet those danc - ing feet on the
a tempo
Em D G Am Em F♯7♭5 Em Cm6 B7♯5 Em C6 B7♯5
av - e - nue I'm tak - ing you to, For - ty - Sec - ond Street.
3fr

Em
B7
Em
B7
Hear the beat of danc - ing feet, it's the
Em
D
G
Am
Em
F♯7♭5
Em
Cm6
3fr
B7♯5
song I love the mel - o - dy of, For - ty - Sec - ond
Em
C7
Street. Lit - tle "nif - ties" from the Fif - ties, in - no - cent and
A9
5fr
A7
sweet; sex - y la - dies from the Eight - ies, who are in - dis -

E♭9
B7
Em
creet. They're side by side, they're glo - ri -
B7
Em
B7
Em
D
G
Am
fied, where the un - der - world can
Em
F♯7♭5
1
Em
Cm6
B7♯5
Em
Am
B7
meet the e - lite, For - ty - Sec - ond Street.
2
Em
Em(maj7)
Em7
Em6
Em
Cm6
B7♯5
Em
naugh - ty, bawd - y, gawd - y, sport - y, For - ty - Sec - ond Street.
rit.
3fr

GOLDFINGER

from GOLDFINGER

Music by JOHN BARRY
Lyrics by LESLIE BRICUSSE
and ANTHONY NEWLEY

Fmaj7 F B♭
beck - ons you to en - ter his web of
E Am F/A Am6 F/A
sin. But don't go in. Gold - en
Em B7 Em
words he will pour in your ear, but his lies can't dis - guise what you
B7♯9 E Cm
fear. For a gold - en girl knows when he's kissed her.
3fr

Gm6
3fr
D♭dim7
F
D♭
It's the kiss of death from Mis - ter Gold - fin - ger.
Fmaj7
B♭
3
Pret - ty girl, be - ware of this heart of
E
1
Am
F/A
gold. This heart is cold.
Am6
F/A
2
Am
F/A
Am6
F/A
Gold - en cold. He loves on - ly

Am F/A Am6 F/A Am F/A
gold, on - ly gold.
Am6 F/A Am F/A Am6 F/A
He loves gold. He loves on - ly
Am F/A Am6 F/A Am F/A
gold, on - ly gold.
Am6 F/A Am F/A Am6 F/A Am6(add9)
4fr
He loves gold. He loves gold.

GREASE

from GREASE

Words and Music by
BARRY GIBB

Moderately, with a beat
Bm E Bm
I solve my prob - lems and I see the light. We got a
mf
E Bm F♯m7
lov - in' thing. We got - ta feed it right.
Em7 D C Bm E Bm
There ain't no dan - ger we can go too far. We start be - liev - in' now that we can

F♯m7
G
be who we are. Grease is the word.
Bm
E
Bm
They think our love is just a grow - in' pain. Why don't they
We take the pres - sure and we throw a - way. Con - ven - tion -
E
Bm
F♯m7
un - der - stand it's just a cry - in' shame?
al - i - ty be - longs to yes - ter - day.
Em7
D
C
Bm
Their lips are ly - ing. On - ly real is real. We stop the
There is a chance that we can make it so far. We start be -

E
Bm
F♯m7
fight right now. We got to be what we feel.
liev - ing now that we can be who we are.
Grease is the word.
Bm
It's got a groove.
Em7
It's got a mean - ing.
Bm
Grease is the time, is the place, is the mo - tion.

Em7
To Coda
1
G
Grease is the way we are feel - ing.
2
G
A
Em7
F#m7
- ing. This is a life of il - lu - sion, wrapped up in trou -
G
F#
Bm
D.S. al Coda
(lyric 2)
- bles, laced in con - fu - sion. What are we do - ing here?
CODA
G
Bm
- ing.

HIGH NOON
(Do Not Forsake Me)
from HIGH NOON

Words by NED WASHINGTON
Music by DIMITRI TIOMKIN

Moderately
N.C.
mp
E♭
3fr
E♭
3fr
Do not for - sake me, oh, my dar - lin',
E♭7
A♭
4fr
Fm
on this, our wed - ding day.
Fm7
B♭7
E♭
3fr
Cm
3fr
Do not for - sake me, oh, my dar - lin'.

G
B♭7
Wait, ___ wait a - long! ___
E♭
I do not know what fate a - waits me. ___
E♭7
A♭
C7
I on - ly know I must be brave ___
Fm
F♯dim7
E♭/G
E♭7
and I must face a man who hates me, ___

A♭ E♭ A♭ E♭
or lie a cow - ard, a cra - ven cow - ard,
A♭ E♭/B♭ A♭/B♭ B♭7 E♭
or lie a cow - ard in my grave!
A♭
Oh, to be torn 'twixt love and du - ty,
E♭ A♭
s'pos - in' I lose my fair - haired beau - ty. Look at the big hand

E♭
A♭
move a - long near - in' high noon. He made a vow while
E♭
A♭m
in state's pris - on, vowed it would be my life or his; 'n' I'm not a - fraid of
E♭
Edim7
Fm7
B♭7
death, but, oh, what will I do if you leave
B♭+
E♭
me? Do not for - sake me, oh, my dar - lin'.

E♭7
A♭
You made that promise as a bride.
C7
Fm
F♯dim7
E♭/G
Do not forsake me, oh, my darlin'.
E♭7
A♭
E♭
A♭
Al - though you're griev - in', don't think of
E♭
A♭
E♭/B♭
A♭/B♭
B♭7
leav - in' now that I need you by my
4fr
3fr
6fr

1
E♭
Fm7/B♭
2
E♭
side!
side!
Wait a -
A♭
E♭
long,
wait a - long,
wait a -
A♭
E♭
long,
wait a - long!
8va
dim.
rall.

THEME FROM ICE CASTLES
(Through the Eyes of Love)
from ICE CASTLES

Music by MARVIN HAMLISCH
Lyrics by CAROLE BAYER SAGER

Slowly, with feeling ♩ = 70
B♭(add9)
C7/B♭
B♭(add9)
Fsus
mp
Dm7
Gm
Fsus
B♭
Please, don't let this feel - ing
now I can take the
Please, don't let this feel - ing
F/B♭
Fm7/B♭
end. It's ev - 'ry - thing I am, ev - 'ry - thing I
time. I can see my life as it comes up
end. It might not come a - gain and I want to re -

E♭maj9 E♭maj7 Dm7 Cm7 Cm7/F F9/E♭ Dm7 Gm7 Dm7
want to be. I can see what's mine now
shin - ing now. Reach-ing out to touch you
mem - ber how it feels to touch you,
Cm7 Cm7/F F7/E♭ Dm7 Gm7 E♭maj7 E♭6 D7sus D7
find - ing out what's true
I can feel so much
how I feel so much
since I found
Gm7 Gm7/F C9/E
To Coda
1
Cm7 Cm7/F
you look-ing through the eyes of love. And

2
Cm7 Cm7/F Bb Gm
3fr 8fr 3fr
through the eyes of love. And now I
Dm7 Gm Dm7 Cm7 Cm7/F Bb
3fr 3fr 8fr
do be-lieve that e-ven in the storm we'll find some light.
Cm7 Dm7 Eb Bb/D C7 Cm7/F
3fr 3fr 8fr
Know-ing you're be-side me, I'm all right.
D.S. al Coda
CODA
Cm7 Cm7/F Bb
3fr 8fr
through the eyes of love.
rit.

JAMES BOND THEME

from DR. NO

By MONTY NORMAN

Moderately bright (♩ = 138)
f
mp
cresc.
mf

With a slight Swing feel
f

Tempo I
mf
p

LAURA
from LAURA

Lyrics by JOHNNY MERCER
Music by DAVID RAKSIN

Slowly, with expression
Am7
D7♭9
G6
Lau - ra is the face in the mist - y light,
mp
Gm7
C7♭9
foot - steps that you hear down the
Fmaj7
F6
Fm7
hall, the laugh

Bb11 Abm6/Bb Bb7b9 Ebmaj7 Eb
4fr 3fr 3fr
that floats on a sum - mer night that you can
Am7b5 D7b5(b9) D9b5 D7 Bm7 G/B
4fr 4fr
nev - er quite re - call.
E9 E7b9 Am7 D7b9
4fr
And you see Lau - ra on the train that is
G6 Gm7
pass - ing through, those eyes,

C7♭9
Fmaj7
F6
how fa - mil - iar they seem.
Fm7
Fdim7
A♭dim7
C/G
She gave your ver - y first kiss to you.
D7/A
D13♭9
D7♯5(♭9)
G9
That was Lau - ra, but she's on - ly a
1
C6
E9
E7♭9
dream.
2
C6
dream.
rall.

LET IT GO

from Disney's Animated Feature FROZEN

Music and Lyrics by KRISTEN ANDERSON-LOPEZ
and ROBERT LOPEZ

Half-time feel, mysterious
Fm
D♭maj7(no3rd)
E♭sus2
p
With pedal
B♭sus
B♭m
Fm
D♭maj7(no3rd)
E♭sus2
B♭sus
B♭
F5
D♭5
The snow glows white on the mountain to - night; not a
E♭
B♭sus
B♭m
Fm
foot - print to be seen. A king - dom of i - so - la -

D♭maj7(no3rd)
4fr
E♭5
6fr
B♭sus
B♭
- tion, and it looks like I'm the queen.
Fm
D♭maj7(no3rd)
4fr
E♭sus2
The wind is howl - ing like this swirl - ing storm in - side.
B♭sus
B♭m
F5
E♭5
6fr
Could - n't keep it in, heav - en knows I
B♭
B♭(sus2/4)
B♭
E♭
3fr
tried.
Don't let them in,
mf

D♭
don't let them see; be the good girl you al - ways have to be.
E♭
3fr
D♭
Con - ceal, don't feel, don't let them know...
cresc.
N.C.
Well, now they know. Let it go,
p
A♭
4fr
E♭
3fr
Fm
let it go; can't hold it back an - y - more.
let it go; I am one with the wind and sky.

D♭
A♭
4fr
E♭
3fr
Let it go, let it go; turn a-way
Let it go, let it go; you'll nev-
Fm
D♭
A♭
4fr
E♭
3fr
and slam the door. I don't care
-er see me cry. Here I stand,
Fm
D♭
what they're going to say; let the
and here I'll stay; let the
To Coda
Cm
3fr
C♭
D♭5
4fr
storm rage on. The cold nev-er both-ered me an-
storm rage on.

Gaining confidence
A♭
4fr
E♭/G
3fr
y - way.
mf
Fm
D♭
E♭
3fr
It's fun - ny how some dis - tance makes ev - 'ry - thing seem small;
B♭m
Fm
E♭
3fr
and the fears that once con - trolled me can't
B♭sus
B♭
E♭
3fr
get to me at all.
It's time to see

D♭
what I can do, to test the lim - its and break through.
E♭
3fr
D♭
No right, no wrong, no rules for me, I'm
D.S. al Coda
N.C.
free! Let it go,
f
CODA
N.C.

My pow - er flur - ries through the air
in - to the ground.
My soul is spi -
ral - ing in fro - zen frac - tals all a - round.
E♭5
6fr
N.C.
And one thought crys - tal - liz - es like an i - cy blast:

F
D♭maj7
I'm nev - er go - ing back; the
f
mf
E♭
3fr
B♭m
D♭
past is in the past! Let it go,
cresc.
A♭
4fr
E♭
3fr
Fm
let it go, and I'll rise like the break of dawn.
ff
D♭
A♭
4fr
E♭
3fr
Let it go, let it go; that per -

Fm
D♭
A♭
E♭
4fr
3fr
- fect girl is gone.
Here I stand in the
Fm
D♭
D♭m
D♭m7
4fr
4fr
light of day;
let the
Cm
C♭
3fr
storm rage on.
The
D♭sus2
4fr
cold nev - er both - ered me an - y - way.
mp

LET THE RIVER RUN

Theme from the Motion Picture WORKING GIRL

Words and Music by
CARLY SIMON

Slowly, freely
C
C/B♭
We're com - ing to the edge, run - ning on the wa - ter,
mf
Am
C
B♭
Am
B♭/C
C
com - ing through the fog, your sons and daugh - ters.
Slowly
A
D
A
Let the riv - er run, let all the dream - ers wake the

F♯m E D F♯m E
na - tion. Come, the new Je - ru - sa -
Moderately
A Bm/A A D/A A
lem. Sil - ver cit - ies
D A F♯m E
rise; the morn - ing lights the streets that lead them. And
D F♯m E A Bm/A
si - rens call them on with a song.

A F♯m B/D♯
4fr
It's ask - ing for the tak - ing,
D(add9) A/C♯ F♯m
2fr
trem - bling, sha - ak - ing.
Oh, my heart is
G E E7/D
ach - ing. We're com - ing to the edge, run - ning on the wa - ter,
E/C♯ E/B E C
com - ing through the fog, your sons and daugh - ters. We, the great and
(D.S.) Instrumental solo

F
C
small, stand on a star and blaze a
Am
G
F
Am
G
trail of de - sire through the dar - kling
C
Dm/C
C
To Coda
dawn.
Solo ends
It's
Am
D/F♯
C/F
3fr
C/E
ask - ing for the tak - ing. Come run with me now; the sky is the col - or of

C/F
C/E
Am
B♭
3fr
Oh, my heart is ach - ing. We're
blue you've nev-er e-ven seen in the eyes of your lov-er.
G
G7/F
G/E
G/D
D.S. al Coda
com-ing to the edge, run - ning on the wa - ter, com-ing through the fog, your sons and daugh-ters.
CODA
Am
D/F♯
F(add9)
ask - ing for the tak - ing, trem - bling,
C/E
Am
B♭
sha - ak - ing. Oh, my heart is ach - ing. We're

G
G7/F
G/E
G/D
com-ing to the edge, run - ning on the wa - ter, com-ing through the fog, your sons and daugh-ters.
C
F
C
Let the riv-er run, let all the dream - ers wake the
Am
G
F
Am
G
na - tion. Come, the new Je - ru - sa -
C
Dm/A
Repeat and Fade
C
Dm/A
C
Dm/A
Optional Ending
C
lem.

LIVE AND LET DIE

from LIVE AND LET DIE

Words and Music by PAUL McCARTNEY
and LINDA McCARTNEY

Slowly
G
Bm
C
D7
D7♭9
4fr
When you were young and your heart was an o - pen book, _
Instrumental
End instrumental
mf
G
Bm
C
C/D
Cm/D
3fr
you used to say live and let live.)
You used to say live and let live.)
(You know you did, you know you did, you know you
G
Bm
C
A
did.) ___ But if this ev - er - chang - ing world in which we live in makes you
3

D
Bb
give in and cry,
say live and let die!
G
C/G
Gdim
G7
Live and let die,
live and let
C/G
die,
live and let die.
Faster
Gm
3fr
ff

To Coda
Reggae feel
C9
8va lower ad lib. till *
G7
What does it mat - ter to ya, when you got a job to do. You got - ta
mf
D7
Em
F
do it well. You got - ta give the oth - er fel - low hell!
Faster
Gm
3fr
*
ff

D.C. al Coda
CODA
Gm
3fr
E♭m/G♭
3fr

MRS. ROBINSON

from THE GRADUATE

Words and Music by
PAUL SIMON

Em
C
Am
for those who pray.
(Hey, hey, hey,
E
To Coda
hey, hey hey.)
1. We'd
E7
like to know a lit - tle bit a - bout you for our files,
A7
A9
5fr
we'd like to help you learn to help your - self.

D7
G
C
Am
Look a-round you, all you see are sym-pa-thet-ic eyes,
E
D7
stroll a-round the grounds un-til you feel at home.
D.S. al Coda
And here's to you,
CODA
E7
2. Hide it in a hid-ing place where
3. Sit-ting on a so-fa on a
no one ev-er goes,
Sun-day af-ter-noon,
A7
put it in your pan-
go-ing to the can-

D7
- try with your cup - cakes, it's a lit - tle se -
- di - dates' de - bate, laugh a - bout it, shout
G C Am
- cret, just the Rob - in - son's af - fair,
a - bout it, when you've got to choose,
E D7
most of all, you've got to hide it from the kids. Coo, coo, ca - choo,
ev - 'ry way you look at it, you lose. Where have you gone,
G Em G Em
Mis - sus Rob - in - son, Je - sus loves you more than you will
Joe Di - Mag - gi - o? A na - tion turns its lone - ly eyes to

C
D7
know. (Wo, wo, wo.) God bless you
you. (Woo, woo, woo.) What's that you
G
Em
G
Em
please, Mis-sus Rob - in - son, Heav-en holds a place for those who pray.
say, Mis-sus Rob - in - son? "Jolt - in' Joe" has left and gone a - way.
C
Am
(Hey, hey, hey, hey, hey, hey.)
(Hey, hey, hey, hey, hey, hey.)
E
1
2
E7(add13)

MOON RIVER

from the Paramount Picture BREAKFAST AT TIFFANY'S

Words by JOHNNY MERCER
Music by HENRY MANCINI

C7/G F B♭9♯11 Am Am7/G
5fr
mak - er, you heart - break - er, wher - ev - er you're
F♯m7♭5 B7 Em7 A7 Dm7 G9 C
4fr
9fr
go - in', I'm go - in' your way. Two
Am F C/E F
drift - ers, off to see the world. There's such a lot of
C/E Bm7♭5 E7 Am
world to see. We're af -

Am/G
F♯m7♭5
4fr
F13
C/E
ter the same rain - bow's end.
F
C/E
F
C/E
wait - in' 'round the bend,
my Huck - le - ber - ry friend,
Am
Dm7
G9
9fr
1
C
Moon Riv - er and me.
2
A♭maj7
D♭maj7
C
me.
rall.

THE MUSIC OF GOODBYE
from OUT OF AFRICA

Words and Music by JOHN BARRY,
ALAN BERGMAN and MARILYN BERGMAN

Medium slow Ballad
F
Em7♭5
A7
Dm
mp
C9
F
Em7♭5
A7
A song I know so well, the mu - sic of good -
Dm
B♭maj7
Dm
bye a - gain. It's there each time we say "Hel - lo."

Am7
Bbmaj7
As always there's no reason why again.
C9
F
Em7b5
A7
You kiss me with your eyes and in your arms I
Dm
Dm/C
Bbmaj7
Dm
fly again. But even as we touch the clouds,
Am7
Bbmaj7
C9
there in the quiet is goodbye again. Perhaps the way I

Dm
Gm7
Dm
hold you makes you a - fraid I'll hold you;
B♭maj7
Dm
Am7
makes you a - fraid to love me.
B♭maj7
C9
F
Love me. As through the night we dance,
Em7♭5
A7
Dm
B♭maj7
the ten - der dance of try a - gain, I hear it play - ing

Dm
Am7
B♭maj7
C9
soft - ly and sad - ly: the mu - sic of good-
1
Dm
B♭maj7
Dm
bye.
C9
2
F
B♭maj7
Per - haps the way I bye. Good-
F
E♭maj7
3fr
C9
F(add9)
bye. Good - bye.
rit.

MY HEART WILL GO ON

(Love Theme from 'Titanic')

from the Paramount and Twentieth Century Fox Motion Picture TITANIC

Music by JAMES HORNER
Lyric by WILL JENNINGS

Moderately
C♯m7
Bsus
A
mp
Bsus
B
C♯m7
Bsus
A
Bsus
B
E
Bsus/F♯
Esus
Ev - 'ry night in my dreams I see you, I
E
B
E
Bsus/F♯
A
feel you, that is how I know you go on.

E
B
Asus2
Far a - cross the dis - tance and spac - es be -
E/B
B
E
B
A
tween us, you have come to show you go on.
𝄋
C♯m
B(add4)
A
Near, far, wher - ev - er you are, __
B
C♯m
B(add9)
A
__ I be - lieve that the heart does go on. ___
4fr
7fr

B
C#m
B
A
Once more you o - pen the door
B
C#m
G#m
A
and you're here in my heart, and my heart will go
To Coda
E/B
B
C#m7
Bsus
A
on and on.
Bsus
B
E
B
Asus2
Love can touch us one time and last for a

E/B B E B A
life - time, and nev - er let go till we're gone.
E B Asus2
Love was when I loved you; one true time I
E/B G♯7/B♯ C♯m G♯m Asus2
hold to. In my life we'll al - ways go on.
D.S. al Coda
CODA
C♯m7 Bsus
on.
4fr

A
B
Bsus
C♯m7
Bsus
A
C♯m/G♯
G♯7/F♯
Fm
E♭
You're here, there's
D♭
E♭
Fm
E♭
nothing I fear and I know that my heart will go
D♭
E♭sus
E♭
Fm
E♭
on. We'll stay for -

D♭
E♭
Fm
ev - er this way.
You are safe in my
Cm7
D♭
A♭/E♭
E♭
A♭
heart, and my heart will go on and on.
decrescendo to end
E♭/A♭
D♭/A♭
E♭/A♭
A♭
Mm.
E♭/A♭
D♭/A♭
A♭(add9)
3fr
4fr
6fr

MY OWN TRUE LOVE

from GONE WITH THE WIND

Words by MACK DAVID
Music by MAX STEINER

E♭sus E♭ E♭/G A♭ A♭+ A♭6
my own true love, at last I've found you,
E♭/B♭ E♭/C B♭ Fm7/B♭ B♭7 E♭ Fm7/B♭ B♭7
my own true love, no lips but yours,
E♭sus E♭ E♭/G A♭ A♭+ A♭6
no arms but yours will ev - er lead me
E♭/B♭ B♭7 E♭ Fm7/E♭ E♭ A♭
through heav - en's door. I roamed the earth

Gm
Fm
Fm/E♭
in search of this,
I knew I'd know you,
Gm
Fm7
B♭7
E♭
Fm7/B♭
B♭7
know you by your kiss.
And by your kiss
E♭sus
E♭
E♭/G
A♭
A♭+
A♭6
you've shown true love,
I'm yours for - ev - er,
E♭/B♭
B♭7
1
E♭
Fm7/B♭
B♭7
2
E♭
Fm7/E♭
E♭
my own true love.
love.
8vb

NIGHT FEVER
from SATURDAY NIGHT FEVER

Words and Music by BARRY GIBB,
ROBIN GIBB and MAURICE GIBB

Moderate Disco beat
Dm7
Gm7
Fmaj7
Gm7
mf
C
Bb
Lis - ten to the ground, there is move - ment all a - round. There is
heat of our love, don't need no help for us to make it. Gim - me
F
C
some - thing go - in' down, and I can feel it. On the
just e - nough to take us to the morn - in.' I got

Dm
waves of the air, there is danc - in' out there. If it's
fire in my mind. I got high - er in my walk - in'. And I'm
F
B♭
C
some - thin' we can share, we can steal it.
glow - in' in the dark; I give you warn - in.'
And that
Am
B♭
sweet cit - y wom - an, she moves through the light, con -
Am
Em
trol - ling my mind and my soul. When you

Am
Dm
A
reach out for me, yeah, and the feel - in' is bright, then I get
Dm7
Gm7
night fe - ver, night fe - ver. We know how to do
Fmaj7
Gm7
it. Gim - me that
Dm7
Gm7
night fe - ver, night fe - ver. We know how to show

Fmaj7
Gm7
it.
G
Dm
G
Here I am, pray - in' for this mo - ment to last,
Dm
G
Dm
liv - in' on the mu - sic so fine,
borne on the wind,
G
Dm
G
D5
5fr
mak - in' it mine.

Dm7
Gm7
Night fe - ver, night fe - ver.
(D.S.) night fe - ver, night fe - ver.
We know how to do
Fmaj7
Gm7
it.
Gim-me that
Dm7
Gm7
Fmaj7
night fe - ver, night fe - ver.
We know how to show it.
1
Gm7
In the
2
Gm7
D.S. and Fade
Gim-me that

THEME FROM "NEW YORK, NEW YORK"

from NEW YORK, NEW YORK

Words by FRED EBB
Music by JOHN KANDER

F
Gm7
C7
shoes are long - ing to stray
Gm7/C
C7
F
Fmaj7
and step a - round the heart of it,
(D.S.) Instrumental
New York, New
F7
E♭/F
F7
B♭maj7
York. I wan - na wake up in the
To Coda
B♭m6
6fr
F
Fmaj7
Gm7
Fmaj7
cit - y that does - n't sleep to find I'm

Am7
D7
Gm7
king of the hill, top of the heap.
C7
F
My lit - tle town blues are melt - ing a -
Gm7
C7
Gm7/C
C7
F
way. I'll make a brand - new start of it
F6
Cm7
3fr
F7
in old New York. If I can

B♭
B♭m6
6fr
F/C
F/A
D7♯5
make it there, I'd make it an - y - where.
D7
C7/E
D7/F♯
Gm7
Am7
B♭maj7
C9sus
It's up to you, New York, New
F
Gm7
York.
f
D.S. al Coda
C7sus
C7
Gm7/C
C7
mf
CODA
Am7
3
king of the hill,

D9
Bbm7
head of the list, cream of the crop at the
Db7
N.C.
Slower
Gb
top of the heap. My lit - tle town blues
molto rit.
f
Abm7
Db7
Ebdim
Fm7b5
are melt - ing a - way. I'll make a
Gb
Gbmaj7
Dbm7
brand - new start of it in old New York.

G♭7
C♭
C♭m6
7fr
If I can make it there, I'd make it
G♭
G♭/B♭
6fr
E♭7♯5
E♭7
D♭7/F
E♭7/G
A♭m7
4fr
B♭m7
an - y - where. Come on, come through, New
C♭6
C♭/D♭
4fr
G♭
York, New York.
ff

NOBODY DOES IT BETTER

from THE SPY WHO LOVED ME

Music by MARVIN HAMLISCH
Lyrics by CAROLE BAYER SAGER

Slowly
C
Cm
No - bod - y does it
No - bod - y does it
mf
G
G7
C
Cm
G
G7
bet - ter; makes me feel sad for the rest.
bet - ter; some - times I wish some - one could.
C
Cm
B7♯5(♭9)
B7♭9
Em7
Am7
Am7/D
D7
No-bod - y does it half as good as you. Ba - by, you're the
No-bod - y does it quite the way you do. Did you have to be so

G
G7
Gdim7
Cm/G
F♯
G
G7/B
best.
good?
I was-n't look - in'
The way that you hold me
C
Cm
G
G7/B
but some-how you found me.
when-ev-er you hold me,
I tried to hide from your
there's some kind of mag - ic in -
A9
A♭9
G
G7/B
love light,
side you
but, like heav-en a - bove me,
that keeps me from run - nin',
C
Cm
B7
E7♭9
Am7
D7
the spy who loved me is keep - in' all my se - crets safe to -
but just keep it com - in'. How'd you learn to do the things you

1
2
G G C Cm
night. do? And no - bod - y does it
G G7 C Cm G G7
bet - ter; makes me feel sad for the rest.
3
C Cm B7#5(b9) B7b9 Em7 Am7 G/B
No - bod - y does it half as good as you. Ba - by, ba - by,
Cmaj7 C#m7b5 C/D G G7 Gdim7 Cm/G F# G
ba - by, you're the best.
3fr
4fr

OVER THE RAINBOW

from THE WIZARD OF OZ

Music by HAROLD ARLEN
Lyric by E.Y. "YIP" HARBURG

E♭
A♭/E♭
E♭maj7
3fr
When all the clouds dark - en up the sky - way, there's a rain - bow high - way to be
Dm7
G7
Cm
A♭7
F9
4fr
found, lead - ing from your win - dow -
Fm7/B♭
E♭
Fm7/B♭
pane to a place be - hind the sun,
E♭
E♭dim
6fr
Fm7/B♭
B♭7
just a step be - yond the rain.
rall.

Eb6 Cm7 Gm Eb7 Ab Abmaj7 Ab7 Gm7 Eb Gm7 Gdim
3fr 3fr 4fr 4fr 3fr
Some - where o - ver the rain - bow way up high,
p - mf
Ab6 Abm6 Eb/Bb C7b9 F7 Fm/Bb Bb7
3fr 4fr 6fr
there's a land that I heard of once in a lull - a -
Eb Fm7 Bb7b9 Eb6 Cm7 Gm Eb7
3fr 3fr 3fr
by. Some - where o - ver the rain - bow
Ab Abmaj7 Ab7 Gm7 Eb Gm7 Gdim Ab6 Abm6 Eb/Bb C7b9
4fr 4fr 3fr 3fr 4fr 6fr
skies are blue, and the dreams that you dare to

F7 Fm/B♭ B♭7 E♭
dreamily
dream real - ly do come true. Some - day I'll wish up - on a star and
Fm/E♭ B♭7/E♭ E♭6 B♭ A♭ E♭ B♭7
wake up where the clouds are far be - hind me. Where
E♭ F♯dim Fm6 F7♭9
trou - bles melt like lem - on drops, a - way, a - bove the chim - ney tops that's where you'll
Fm7/B♭ B♭9♯5 E♭6 Cm7 Gm E♭7 A♭ A♭maj7 A♭7
find me. Some - where o - ver the rain - bow blue - birds

Gm7 Eb Gm7 Gdim Ab6 Abm6 Eb/Bb C7b9 F7 Fm/Bb Bb7
fly. Birds fly o - ver the rain - bow, why then, oh why can't
Eb Bb9 Bb7b9 Eb6 Eb
1
2
I? I?
rall.
Fm7/Eb Eb Fm7 Bb7
If
Eb Fm7 Bb7 Eb6
hap - py lit - tle blue - birds fly be - yond the rain - bow, why oh why can't I?
rit.
pp
L.H.

THE RAINBOW CONNECTION

from THE MUPPET MOVIE

Words and Music by PAUL WILLIAMS
and KENNETH L. ASCHER

Moderately, with a lilt
A
D/A
A
D/A
mp
A
F♯m
F♯m7
Bm
D/E
E
Why are there so man - y songs a - bout rain - bows, and
Who said that ev - 'ry wish would be heard and an - swered when
A
E/G♯
F♯m7
A/E
D(add2)
D/E
Esus
what's on the oth - er side?
wished on the morn - ing star?
A
E/F♯
F♯m7
Bm7
D/E
E
Rain - bows are vi - sions, but on - ly il - lu - sions, and
Some - bod - y thought of that, and some - one be - lieved it;

A E/G♯ F♯m7 A/E D(add2) D(add2)/A
7fr
rain - bows have noth - ing to hide.
look what it's done so far.
Dmaj7
So we've been told, and some choose to be - lieve it.
What's so a - maz - ing that keeps us star - gaz - ing, and
G♯m/C♯
4fr
I know they're wrong; wait and see.
what do we think we might see?
Bm7 E D/E C♯m7 E/F♯ F♯7
4fr
Some - day we'll find it, the Rain - bow Con - nec - tion; the
Some - day we'll find it, the Rain - bow Con - nec - tion; the

Bm7 E7sus E7
1 A D/A
lov - ers, the dream - ers and me.
lov - ers, the dream - ers and
A D/A
2 A E/G♯
me. All of us
F♯m7 A/E D(add2) A/C♯
un - der its spell; we know that it's prob - a - bly
D6/E E♭6/F F(add2) F B♭
mag - ic.
Have you been

F/G Gm7 Cm7 E♭/F F B♭ F/A
half a - sleep and have you heard voic - es? I've heard them
Gm7 B♭/F E♭(add2) E♭/F Fsus B♭ F/G Gm7
call - ing my name. Is this the sweet sound that
Cm7 E♭/F F B♭ F/A Gm7 E♭(add2)
calls the young sail - ors? The voice might be one and the same.
E♭ E♭maj7
I've heard it too man - y times to ig -
3fr
6fr

Am/D
nore it. It's some - thing that I'm s'posed to be.
Cm7 F E♭/F Dm7 F/G G7
Some - day we'll find it, the Rain - bow Con - nec - tion; the
Cm7 F7sus F7 B♭ F/A Gm7
lov - ers, the dream - ers and me. La da da dee da da
B♭/F E♭(add2) E♭ Fsus F7 B♭
do la la da da da de da do.

RAINDROPS KEEP FALLIN' ON MY HEAD

from BUTCH CASSIDY AND THE SUNDANCE KID

Lyric by HAL DAVID
Music by BURT BACHARACH

Fmaj7 F7 B♭ Am7 D7
sun. And I said I did-n't like the way he got things done. Sleep-in'on the
Am7 D7 Gm7 B♭/C C
job. Those rain-drops are fall-in'on my head. They keep fall-in'! But there's one
F Fmaj7 B7 B♭ C C7
thing I know: the blues they send to meet me won't de-feat
Am7 D9
me. It won't be long till hap-pi-ness steps up
4fr

Gm7 Bb/C C Bb/C C F
to greet me.
Raindrops keep fall-in' on my
Fmaj7 F7 Bb Am7 D7
head, but that does-n't mean my eyes will soon be turn-in' red. Cry-in's not for
Am7 D7 Gm7
me 'cause I'm nev-er gon-na stop the rain by com-plain-in'.
Bb/C C F Fmaj7 Gm7 Bb/C F
Be-cause I'm free, noth-in's wor-ry-in' me.

THE ROSE

from the Twentieth Century-Fox Motion Picture Release THE ROSE

Words and Music by
AMANDA McBROOM

C G F C
love, it is a flow - er, and you, its on - ly seed.
a tempo
It's the heart a - fraid of break - ing that
night has been too lone - ly and the
G
F G C G
nev - er learns to dance. It's the dream a - fraid of wak - ing that
road has been too long, and you think that love is on - ly for the
F G C Em/B Em
nev - er takes the chance. It's the one who won't
luck - y and the strong, just re - mem - ber in the
f

Am7
Am7/G
5fr
F
G
be tak - en, who can - not seem to give, and the
win - ter far be - neath the bit - ter snows lies the
mf
C
G
1
F
G
soul a - fraid of dy - in' that nev - er learns to
seed that with the sun's love in the
C
2
F
G
live. When the spring be - comes the
C
rose.
(Vocal 1st time only)

SINGIN' IN THE RAIN

from SINGIN' IN THE RAIN

Lyric by ARTHUR FREED
Music by NACIO HERB BROWN

G6
G♯dim7
D7/A
D7
glo - ri - ous feel - ing, I'm hap - py a -
gain. I'm laugh - ing at clouds so
dark up a - bove, the sun's in my
G6
heart and I'm read - y for love. Let the

storm - y clouds chase ev - 'ry - one from the
place. Come on with the rain, I've a
G♯dim7
D7/A
D7
smile on my face. I'll walk down the
lane with a hap - py re - frain, and

G6
Fine
sing - in', just sing - in' in the rain.
E♭7
G6
Why am I smil - in' and why do I sing?
E♭7
G6
Why does De - cem - ber seem sun - ny as Spring?
D7
G6
Why do I get up each morn - ing to start

E7
A7
Hap - py and head up with joy in my heart?
Bb7
Why is each new task a
Eb
3fr
F7
tri - fle to do?
Be - cause I am
Eb7
D7
D.S. al Fine
liv - ing a life full of you.
I'm

ST. ELMO'S FIRE
(Man in Motion)
from the Motion Picture ST. ELMO'S FIRE

Words by JOHN PARR
Music by DAVID FOSTER

A/C♯
D
A
mov - in' straight a - head, you knew it all.
on - ly you can do what must be done.
on - ly just a few miles down the road.
F♯m7
D
But may - be some - time, if you feel the pain, you'll find you're
You know, in some way you're a lot like me. You're just a
And I can make it, I know I can. You broke the
1
F♯m7
D
E
all a - lone; ev - 'ry - thing has changed.
2, 3
F♯m7
D
E
pris - on - er, and you're try'n' to break free.
boy in me, but you won't break the man.

F♯
Bsus2
C♯sus
C♯
I can see a new ho - ri - zon un - der - neath the blaz - ing sky.
F♯
B
C♯sus
C♯
I'll be where the ea - gle's fly - ing high - er and high - er.
F♯
Bsus2
C♯sus
C♯
Gon - na be a man in mo - tion. All I need's this pair of wheels.
To Coda
F♯
B
C♯sus
C♯
D
Take me where the fu - ture's ly - ing: St. El - mo's fire.

Ddim7
C♯7
A
D.S. al Coda
(take 2nd ending)
CODA
B
C♯sus
C♯
F♯
St. El - mo's fire. I can climb the high - est moun - tain,
Bsus2
C♯sus
C♯
F♯
cross the wild - est sea. I can feel St. El - mo's fire
B
C♯sus
C♯
D
Ddim7
burn - ing in me, burn - ing in me,

A
Dsus2/F♯
E
A
Just once in his life
Dsus2/F♯
a man has his
E
time,
A
and my time is
now!
Dsus2/F♯
I'm com - in' a - live!
E

F♯
Bsus2
C♯sus
C♯
4fr
I can hear the mu - sic play - in'; I can see the ban - ners fly.
I can see a new ho - ri - zon un - der-neath the blaz - ing sky.
F♯
B
C♯sus
C♯
3
Feel like a vet a - gain; I hope I ain't high.
I'll be where the ea - gle's fly - ing high - er and high - er.
F♯
Bsus2
C♯sus
C♯
Gon - na be a man in mo - tion. All I need's this pair of wheels.
Repeat and Fade
Optional Ending
F♯
B
C♯sus
C♯
F♯
Take me where the fu - ture's ly - ing: St. El - mo's fire.

SECRET LOVE
from CALAMITY JANE

Words by PAUL FRANCIS WEBSTER
Music by SAMMY FAIN

Freely
B♭7
E♭6/G
E♭m6/G♭
Fm7
Fm7/E♭
B♭9sus
B♭9
mp
rit.
Moderately, with much tenderness
E♭6
Fm7
B♭7
E♭6
Once I had a se - cret love that lived with -
So I told a friend - ly star, the way that
Fm7/B♭
B♭7
Fm7/B♭
B♭7
Fm7
in the heart of me. All too
dream - ers of - ten do, just how
B♭9/F
Fm7
B♭7/F
Fm7
B♭7/F
B♭7
soon my se - cret love be - came im - pa - tient to be
won - der - ful you are and why I'm so in love with

1
Eb6 Fm7 Bb7
free.
2
Eb6 Cm
you. Now I
F7/A Bb Dm Bbm7/Eb Eb7/G
shout it from the high - est hills, e - ven told the gold - en
Ab Abm Eb/G Eb Gm7b5 C7#5(b9) C7b9
daf - fo - dils. At last my heart's an o - pen door, and
Fm7 Bb9sus Bb7b9 Eb6 Abmaj7 Fm7 Eb6
my se - cret love's no se - cret an - y - more.
rall.

SKYFALL

from the Motion Picture SKYFALL

Words and Music by ADELE ADKINS
and PAUL EPWORTH

Gsus G Cm A♭ F7 Fm7
For this is the end. I've drowned and dreamt this
Cm A♭ F7 Fm7 Cm A♭
mo - ment. So o - ver - due I owe them.
F7 Fm7 Cm/D Gsus G
Swept a - way, I'm stol - en. Let the
Cm Cm/B♭ A♭ Cm/G Fm7 Fm/E♭
sky fall. When it crum - bles, we will stand tall, face it all
3fr
4fr
8fr

Dm7♭5 G7 Cm Cm/B♭ A♭ Cm/G
together. Let the sky fall. When it crumbles, we will
To Coda
F7 D7♯9 G7 Cm A♭ F7 Fm7
stand tall, face it all together at skyfall. At sky-
Cm A♭ F7 Fm7 Cm A♭ F7 Fm7
fall. Sky-fall is where we start, a thou-sand miles and
Cm A♭ F7 Fm7 Cm A♭
poles a-part. When worlds col-lide and days are dark. You may have my

F7
Fm7
Cm/D
Gsus
G
D.S. al Coda
num - ber, you can take my name but you'll nev - er have my heart. Let the
CODA
Cm
fall. Let the sky fall. When it crum - bles, we will stand tall.
Let the sky fall. When it crum - bles,
F9
we will stand tall. Where you go, I go. What you see,

A♭maj7
Cm/B♭
Cm/B
Cm
Cm/B♭
8fr
3fr
I see. I know I'll nev-er be me with-out the se-cu-ri-ty of your
A♭maj7
Cm/G
Fm7
Cm/E♭
Cm/D
lov-ing arms keep-ing me from harm. Put your hand in my hand and we'll
Gsus
G
Cm
Cm/B♭
A♭
Cm/G
4fr
stand. Let the sky fall. When it crum-bles, we will
Fm7
Fm/E♭
Dm7♭5
G7
Cm
Cm/B♭
stand tall, face it all to-geth-er. Let the sky fall. When it

A♭ Cm/G F7 D7♯9 G7
4fr 3fr 4fr
crum - bles, we will stand tall, face it all to-geth-er at sky -
Cm Cm/B♭ A♭ Cm/G Fm7 A♭/E♭
3fr 8fr 4fr 3fr
fall. Let the sky fall. We will stand tall
Dm7♭5 Cm/D G7 Cm Cm/B♭ A♭ Cm/G
3fr 3fr 8fr 4fr 3fr
at sky - fall,
F9(no3rd) G Cm(add9)
8fr
ooh.

SOME DAY MY PRINCE WILL COME

from Walt Disney's SNOW WHITE AND THE SEVEN DWARFS

Words by LARRY MOREY
Music by FRANK CHURCHILL

Dm7 G7 B♭/C C7
some - one who'll thrill me for - ev - er.
rall.
F A7♯5 B♭ D7
Some day my prince will come,
Some day I'll find my love,
a tempo
Gm 3fr Gm/F C7 F
some day I'll find my love, and how thrill - ing that
some - one to call my own, and I'll know her the
G♯dim7 Gm7 C7 F G♯dim7
mo - ment will be, when the prince of my dreams comes to
mo - ment we meet, for my heart will start skip - ping a

Gm7 C7 F A7♯5 B♭
me. He'll whis - per "I love
beat. Some day we'll say and
D7 Gm Gm/F C7
you," and steal a kiss or two. Though he's
do things we've been long - ing to. Though she's
F A7 A+ B♭+ Bdim7 F F♯dim7
far a - way, I'll find my love some day, some day when my
Gm7 C7
1
F A♭m6 Gm7 B♭/C C7
2
F6
dreams come true. true.
rall.
3fr
4fr

SOMEWHERE
from WEST SIDE STORY

Lyrics by STEPHEN SONDHEIM
Music by LEONARD BERNSTEIN

B♭/D B♭7 E♭7 A♭ Fm7 B♭7/D E♭7 A♭
4fr
There's a time for us, Some - day a time for us.
B♭ B♭/A♭ Gm Cm A♭ D♭ B♭m G♭
3fr 3fr 4fr
3
cresc.
Time to-geth - er with time to spare, Time to learn, time to care.
cresc.
C♭ A♭m E♭m E♭m6
4fr 6fr
mf
f
Some - day, some - where We'll find a new way of
Fm7 C♭/E♭ Fm7♭5 G♭maj7
4fr
p
liv - ing, We'll find a way of for - giv - ing,

F Dm7 Bb Bb7/D Eb7 Ab
rit.
pp a tempo
some-where. There's a place for us,
Fm7 Bb7/D Eb7 Ab Bb Bb/Ab Gm Cm
A time and place for us. Hold my hand and we're half - way there.
cresc.
Ab Db Bbm Gb Cb
f
Hold my hand and I'll take you there, some - how,
mf
Abm Eb Eb7 Ab/Eb Ebsus2 Eb
some - day, some - where.
pp

SOMEWHERE, MY LOVE

Lara's Theme from DOCTOR ZHIVAGO

Lyric by PAUL FRANCIS WEBSTER
Music by MAURICE JARRE

Am7 D7 Am7 D7 G
and there are dreams, all that your heart can hold.
C G
Some - day we'll meet a - gain, my love.
B♭ F B♭ D7
Some - day when - ev - er the spring breaks through.
G Gdim D7
You'll come to me out of the long a - go,

Am7 D7 Am7 D7 G
warm as the wind, soft as the kiss of snow.
Gdim D7
Till then, my sweet, think of me now and then.
(Lar - a, my own,)
Am7 D7
God - speed, my love,
1
Am7 D7 G
'til you are mine a - gain.
2
Am7 D7 D7♭9 G
'til you are mine a - gain.
4fr

SOMEWHERE OUT THERE

from AN AMERICAN TAIL

Music by BARRY MANN and JAMES HORNER
Lyric by CYNTHIA WEIL

Moderately, with expression
C Cmaj7/E C/F G7sus C C/E F(add9)
mp
With pedal
Dm G/F Em7 Am7 F G
C(add9) Cmaj7/E C/F F/G C(add9) C/E
mf
Some - where out there, be - neath the pale moon -
F Dm7 G/F Em Am
light, some - one's think - in' of me and

Dm7 C/E F Gsus G C(add9) Cmaj7/E
3fr
lov - ing me to - night. Some - where out
C/F F/G C(add9) C/E F
3fr
there, some - one's say - ing a prayer that
Dm7 G/F Em7 Am Dm7 C/E F/G
we'll find one an - oth - er in that big some - where out
C F G/F F G/F
there. And e - ven though I know how ver - y far a - part we are it

Fmaj7
G/F
F
G/F
helps to think we might be wish - in' on the same bright star. And
A♭
4fr
B♭/A♭
A♭
4fr
B♭/A♭
when the night wind starts to sing a lone - some lull - a - by it
A♭
4fr
B♭/A♭
G
helps to think we're sleep - ing un - der - neath the same big sky.
To Coda
C
Cmaj7/E
Fmaj9
F/G
C
C/E
Some - where out there if love can see us

F Dm7 G/F Em7 Am7 F
through, then we'll be to - geth - er some - where out there, out
G C D/C C D/C C/B♭ B♭maj7
where dreams come true.
Am/B♭ D/E A C♯m7
4fr
A/D D/E A A/C♯ D D+ D6 A/C♯

Bm7 Dmaj7 C♯m F♯m7 Bm7 C♯m D/E
A
D.S. al Coda
And
CODA
C C/E F
love can see us through,
(love can see us
Dm G/F Em7 Am F G
then we'll be to - geth - er some-where out there, out where dreams come
through)
C Cmaj7/E C/F G7sus C(add9)
true.
rit.

SPEAK SOFTLY, LOVE
(Love Theme)
from the Paramount Picture THE GODFATHER

Words by LARRY KUSIK
Music by NINO ROTA

Slowly
Cm
Fm6/C
mp
Fm/C
Cm/E♭
Fm
Cm/G
G7sus
G7
3fr
Speak soft - ly, love, and hold me warm a - gainst your heart. I feel your
words, the ten - der, trem - bling mo - ments start. We're in a world our ver - y
own, shar - ing a love that on - ly few have ev - er known. Wine - col - ored

Bb7/D
Bb7
Eb
3fr
Db/F
Fm6/Ab
6fr
days warmed by the sun, deep vel - vet nights when we are
3
G
N.C.
Cm
Fm/C
one. Speak soft - ly, love, so no one hears us but the sky. The vows of
Fm/C
Cm
Fm6/C
Fm
love we make will live un - til we die. My life is yours and all be -
Cm
Cm/G
G7sus
G7
1
2
cause you came in - to my world with love so soft - ly, love. Speak soft - ly, love.
rit.

STAR WARS
(Main Theme)
from STAR WARS, THE EMPIRE STRIKES BACK and RETURN OF THE JEDI

Music by JOHN WILLIAMS

Majestically, steady March (♩ = 108)
f
poco rall.
a tempo
legato

mp
marc.
poco rall.
f a tempo
simile

mf
simile

simile

STAYIN' ALIVE

from the Motion Picture SATURDAY NIGHT FEVER

Words and Music by BARRY GIBB,
ROBIN GIBB and MAURICE GIBB

Medium Rock beat
Fm7
Well, you can tell
f
Eb
Fm
by the way I use my walk, I'm a wom - an's man: no time to talk.
get low and I get high, and if I can't get ei - ther, I real - ly try. Got the
Fm7
Eb
Fm
Mu - sic loud and wom - en warm, I've been kicked a - round since I was born. And now it's
wings of heav - en on my shoes. I'm a danc - in' man and I just can't lose. You know it's

B♭7
all right. It's O - K. And you may look the oth - er way.
all right. It's O - K. I'll live to see an - oth - er day.
We can try to un - der - stand the New York Times' ef - fect on man.
Fm7
Wheth - er you're a broth - er or wheth - er you're a moth - er, you're stay - in' a - live, stay - in' a - live.
Feel the cit - y break - in' and ev - 'ry - bod - y shak - in' and we're stay - in' a - live, stay - in' a - live.

Ah, ha, ha, ha, stay-in' a-live, stay-in' a-live. Ah, ha, ha, ha,
Fm
Eb/F
Fm
stay-in' a-live.
Cm7
To Coda
1
Fm7
Well now, I
2
Fm7
Bb7
Life go-in' no-where.

Fm7
Some-bod-y help me.
Some-bod-y help me, yeah.
B♭7
Life go-in' no-where.
Some-bod-y help me, yeah.
Fm7
D.S. al Coda
(Verse 1)
Stay-in' a-live.
Well, you can tell
CODA
Fm7

B♭7
Life go - in' no - where.
Some - bod - y help me.
Fm7
Some - bod - y help me, yeah.
B♭7
Life go - in' no - where.
Some - bod - y help me, yeah.
Fm7
I'm stay - in' a - live.
Repeat and Fade

SUDDENLY
from LES MISÉRABLES

Music by CLAUDE-MICHEL SCHÖNBERG
Lyrics by HERBERT KRETZMER and ALAIN BOUBLIL

G
C/G
G
gun.
Sud - den - ly the world
Nev - er - more a - lone,
a tempo
C/G
G
C/E
seems a diff-'rent place, some - how full of grace, full of light.
nev - er - more a - part, you have warmed my heart like the sun.
B7
Em7
A9
5fr
G/D
To Coda
How was I to know that so much hope was held in - side me? What is past, is gone.
You have brought the gift of life and love so long de - nied me. Sud - den - ly I see
rit.
a tempo
A little faster
C/D
G
B7
Now we jour - ney on through the night.
How was I to know, at last, that
poco rall.

Em/B
D7
G
hap - pi - ness can come so fast? Trust-ing me the way you do, I'm so a - fraid of fail - ing you.
F♯7♭9
F♯7♭9/A♯
3fr
5fr
Bm
Bm/D
A/C♯
A7
Just a child who can - not know that dan - ger fol - lows where I go. There are shad-ows ev - 'ry-where and
rit.
Dsus
D
D+
D.S. al Coda
mem - o - ries I can - not share.
CODA
Em7
what I could not see.
Am7
C/D
G
C/G
G
Some-thing sud-den-ly has be - gun.
f rall.
p a tempo
rit.

(Theme from)
A SUMMER PLACE
from A SUMMER PLACE

Words by MACK DISCANT
Music by MAX STEINER

Slowly
B♭
Gm7
Cm7
3fr
F7
mp
Bells will be ring - ing and birds will be sing - ing if you and your lov - er should
ev - er dis - cov - er that
there's
There's
a sum - mer
place
where it may
rain
or
B♭maj7

Cm7 F7 B♭maj7 Cm7 F7
3fr
3fr
storm. Yet I'm safe and warm. For with -
B♭ Gm7 Cm7 F7 B♭ Gm7
3fr
in that sum - mer place
Cm7 F7 B♭maj7 Cm7 F7
3fr
3fr
your arms reach out to me and my
B♭maj7 Cm7 F7 B♭ Gm7
3fr
heart is free from all care.

Cm7 F7 Bb Gm7 Cm7 F7
For it knows there are
Gm Dm/F Eb Cm7 Bb/D Gm7 C11 Ebm6
no gloom-y skies when seen through the eyes of
Bb/F Cm/F C9 F9
those who are blessed with love. And the sweet se - cret
Bb Gm7 Cm7 F7 Bb Gm7 Cm7 F7
of a sum - mer place is that it's

B♭maj7 Cm7 F7 B♭maj7
an - y - where when two peo - ple
Cm7 F7 B♭ Gm7 Cm7 F7
share all their hopes, all their
B♭ Gm7 Cm7 F7
dreams, all their love.
1 B♭ Gm Cm7 E♭/F
2 B♭ Gm Cm7 E♭/F B♭6/9
love.

TAKE MY BREATH AWAY
(Love Theme)
from the Paramount Picture TOP GUN

Words and Music by GIORGIO MORODER
and TOM WHITLOCK

Moderately slow
A♭
4fr
Cm/G
3fr
mf
Fm
Cm/G
3fr
A♭
4fr
Watch - ing ev - 'ry mo - tion in
Watch - ing, I keep wait - ing, still
Watch - ing ev - 'ry mo - tion in
Cm/G
3fr
Fm
Cm/G
3fr
my fool - ish lov - er's game;
an - tic - i - pat - ing love,
this fool - ish lov - er's game;

A♭
Cm/G
Fm
on this end - less o - cean, fi - n'lly lov - ers know no shame.
nev - er hes - i - tat - ing to be - come the fat - ed ones.
haunt - ed by the no - tion some - where there's a love in flames.
Cm/G
B♭m
D♭/A♭
Turn - ing and re - turn - ing to some se - cret place in - side;
Turn - ing and re - turn - ing to some se - cret place to hide;
Turn - ing and re - turn - ing to some se - cret place in - side;
E♭
A♭
watch - ing in slow mo - tion as
watch - ing in slow mo - tion as
watch - ing in slow mo - tion as

Cm/G
3fr
D♭
E♭
3fr
you turn a - round and say,
you turn my way and say,
you turn to me and say,
"Take my breath a -
A♭
4fr
Cm/G
3fr
To Coda
1
D♭
way."
E♭
3fr
A♭
4fr
Cm/G
3fr
"Take my breath a - way."
D♭
E♭
3fr
2
Fm

Cm/G
Ab
Bb
Eb/G
Through the hour - glass I saw you. In time,
Db
Ab
Bb
you slipped a - way. When the mir - ror crashed, I called
Eb/G
Db
Ab
you and turned to hear you say, "If on - ly for to -
Bb
Eb
day, I am un - a - fraid.

A♭
4fr
Cm/G
3fr
Take my breath a - way."
Fm
1
Cm/G
3fr
2
Cm/G
3fr
D.S. al Coda
"Take my breath a -
CODA
D♭
E♭
3fr
A♭
4fr
My love, take my breath a - way.
Cm/G
3fr
D♭
E♭
3fr
Repeat and Fade
My love, take my breath a -

THAT'S WHAT FRIENDS ARE FOR

from NIGHT SHIFT

Music by BURT BACHARACH
Words by CAROLE BAYER SAGER

E♭maj9
Gm7
Cm7
Fm7
if I should ev - er go a - way, well, then close your eyes and try
then, for the times when we're a - part, well, then close your eyes and know
Dm7(no5th)
5fr
G7sus
G7
Cm7
3fr
A♭maj7
to feel the way we do to - day,
these words are com - ing from my heart,
and then if you can re - mem -
Fm7/B♭
B♭11
E♭maj9
E♭maj9/D
- ber:
Keep smil - ing, keep shin - ing
A♭maj7/C
B♭/A♭
Gm7
Cm7
3fr
know - ing you can al - ways count on me for sure.

A♭maj7
Fm7/B♭
B♭9
E♭maj9
E♭maj9/D
That's what friends are for.
For good times and bad times,
In good times, in bad times,
D♭6(no5th)
C7sus
C7
C♭6(no5th)
7fr
B♭7sus
To Coda
I'll be on your side for-ev - er - more.
That's what friends are
1
B♭7sus
for.
2
B♭7sus
D.S. al Coda
for.
3
CODA
B♭7sus
for.
Repeat and Fade
E♭maj9
E♭maj9
A♭(add2)/C
Gm7
Cm7
3fr
Fm7
B♭11
Vocal ad lib.

THANKS FOR THE MEMORY

from the Paramount Picture BIG BROADCAST OF 1938

Words and Music by LEO ROBIN
and RALPH RAINGER

B♭6
B♭m6/D♭
2fr
C7
C13
2fr
love - ly it was! Thanks for the
love - ly it was! Thanks for the
F6
F♯dim7
mem - o - ry of rain - y af - ter - noons,
mem - o - ry of lin - ge - rie with lace,
3
C7/G
F/A
D♯dim7
C7/E
swing - y Har - lem tunes, and mo - tor trips and burn - ing lips and
Pils - ner by the case, and how I jumped the day you trumped my
F♯dim7
Gm7
Adim7
B♭6
burn - ing toast and prunes. How love - ly it
one and on - ly ace. How love - ly it

B♭m6/D♭ C7 E♭7/B♭ A♭ E♭9
2fr 6fr 4fr
was! Man - y's the time that we feast - ed and
was! We said good - bye with a high - ball; then
A♭ Adim7 C/G Am
4fr
man - y's the time that we fast - ed. Oh, well, it was swell while it
I got as "high" as a stee - ple. But we were in - tel - li - gent
Dm Fm6/C G7 Gm7 Gm7♭5 C7 C+ D♭dim7
last - ed; we did have fun and no harm done. And
peo - ple; no tears, no fuss, hur - ray for us. So
a tempo
C13 F6 F♯dim7
2fr
thanks for the mem - o - ry of sun-burns at the shore,
thanks for the mem - o - ry and strict - ly en - tre - nous,

C7/G F/A D♯dim7 C7/E
nights in Sing - a - pore. You might have been a head - ache, but you
dar - ling, how are you? And how are all the lit - tle dreams that
1
F♯dim7 Gm7 Adim7 B♭6 C7 F C7♯5 C7
nev - er were a bore, so thank you so much.
2
F♯dim7 Gm7 G♯dim7 F/A
nev - er did come true? Awf - 'ly glad I met you, chee - ri -
D♭7/A♭ Gm7 C7 D♭ F6
o and too - dle - oo, and thank you so much!

A TIME FOR US
(Love Theme)
from the Paramount Picture ROMEO AND JULIET

Words by LARRY KUSIK and EDDIE SNYDER
Music by NINO ROTA

Slowly and expressively
Gm
Cm6
Dm7
Gm
A time for
mf
Dm/F
E♭
B♭/D
us some - day there'll be when chains are torn by cour - age
Cm
Gm
Dm/F
born of a love that's free. A time when dreams so long de -

E♭ Cm Dm Gm
nied can flour - ish as we un - veil the
Dm Gm B♭ F
love we now must hide. A time for us at
Cm Gm A♭ E♭
last to see a life worth - while for
Dm Gm Dm/F
you and me. And with our love through tears and
3fr
4fr

E♭
3fr
B♭/D
Cm
3fr
thorns we will en - dure as we pass sure - ly through ev - 'ry
Gm
3fr
Dm/F
E♭
3fr
storm. A time for us some - day there'll be a
Cm
3fr
Dm
Gm
3fr
new world, a world of shin - ing
Dm
1
Gm
3fr
2
Gm
3fr
hope for you and me. A time for me.
rall.

TO SIR, WITH LOVE

from TO SIR, WITH LOVE

Words by DON BLACK
Music by MARC LONDON

Moderately
C
G7
C
G7
mf
C
D
Those school girl days of tell - ing
The time has come for clos - ing
Those awk - ward years have hur - ried
F
C
tales and bit - ing nails are gone,
books, and long last looks must end.
by. Why did they fly a - way?

D
but in my mind I know they
And as I leave, I know that
Why is it, sir, chil - dren grow
F
C
will still live on and on.
I am leav - ing my best friend.
up to be peo - ple one day?
B7
Em
But how do you thank some - one who has
A friend who taught me right from wrong and
What takes the place of climb - ing trees and
B7
Em
D
tak - en you from cray - ons to per - fume. It is - n't
weak from strong, that's a lot to learn. What can I
dirt - y knees in the world out - side? What is there

G
D
A7
eas - y but I'll try.
give you in re - turn?
for you I can buy?
If you
If you
If you
D
C/D
D
want - ed the sky I'd write a - cross the sky in let - ters that would
want - ed the moon I would try to make a start, but
want - ed the world I'd sur - round it with a wall; I'd scrawl these
C/D
D
G
soar a thou - sand feet high "To sir, with
I would rath - er you let me give my heart to sir, with
words with let - ters ten feet tall: "To sir, with
1, 2
A7
C6
Dm7
G7
3
A7
D
D6/9
4fr
love."
love.
love."

TIME WARP

from THE ROCKY HORROR PICTURE SHOW

Words and Music by
RICHARD O'BRIEN

B
close - ly, not for ver - y much long -
men - sion, with voy - eur - is - tic in - ten -
G
D
er, I've got to keep con -
tion, well se - clud - ed, I'll see
A
trol. I re - mem - ber
all. With a bit of a mind flip
B
do - ing the Time Warp,
you're in - to the time slip.

G
D
A
drink - ing those moments when
Noth - ing can ev - er be the same.
the black - ness hit me
You're spaced out on sen - sa - tion
and the void would be
like you're un - der se -
B
F
C
ALL:
call - ing.
da - tion.
Let's do the
G
D
A
Time Warp a - gain.

F C G D A
Let's do the Time Warp a - gain.
1
N.C.
NARRATOR:
E7
It's just a jump to the left
ALL:
and then a step to the right.
A
N.C.
NARRATOR:
E7
With your hands on your hips,
ALL:
A
you bring your knees in tight.
But it's the pel - vic

D
A
thrusts, that real - ly drive you in - sane.
F
C
G
D
A
Let's do the Time Warp a - gain.
F
C
G
D
A
Let's do the Time Warp a - gain.
MAGENTA:
It's so
2
COLUMBIA:
Well, I was tap - ping down the street, just - a

hav-ing a think, when a snake of a guy gave me an e-vil wink. It
D
shook me up, it took me by sur-prise, had a
A
pick-up truck and the
dev-il's eyes. He
E
stared at me, and I
D
felt a change.
A
Time meant noth-ing; nev-er would a - gain.
F
ALL:
Let's
C
do the

G D A F C
Time Warp a - gain.
Let's do the
G D A
N.C.
NARRATOR:
Time Warp a - gain.
It's just a jump to the left
E7 A
ALL:
and then a step to the right.
N.C.
NARRATOR:
E7
ALL:
With your hands on your hips,
you bring your knees in

A
D
tight.
But it's the pel - vic
thrusts,
A
that real - ly drive you in - sane.
F C G D A
Let's do the Time Warp a - gain.
F C G D A
A7
Let's do the Time Warp a - gain.

TONIGHT
from WEST SIDE STORY

Lyrics by STEPHEN SONDHEIM
Music by LEONARD BERNSTEIN

The complete number, "Balcony Scene," is a duet for Maria and Tony, adapted here as a solo.

B(add2)
C♯(add2)/B
B(add2)
night, to - night, I'll see my love to -
C♯m7/E
C♯m7/D♯
C♯m(add2)
C♯m(add2)/B
A♯m7♭5
night. And for us stars will stop where they
E♭
E♭/D♭
F♭/C♭
are! To - day the
F♭6/C♭
B♭m7♭5
B♭m7♭5/D♭
min - utes seem like hours, the hours go so

Cbm/D
Cbdim7
Bb
Bb/F
slow - ly And still the sky is light.
Bb7/Fb
Ab(add2)/Eb
Ab(add2)
4fr
Bb(add2)/Ab
3fr
O moon, grow bright, And
Ab(add2)
4fr
Ab(add2)/G
Fm(add2)
Cm
3fr
make this end - less day end - less night
Eb7sus/Bb
6fr
Ab
4fr
Fm/Ab
to - night!
cresc.
f

Dm7♭5
D7/A
Good
mp
G/D
A/D
G/D
night, good night, Sleep well and when you
pp
Em
B
D7sus/A
dream, Dream of me To -
f
pp
G
G7
C/G
G
night.
f
p

THE TROLLEY SONG

from MEET ME IN ST. LOUIS

Words and Music by HUGH MARTIN
and RALPH BLANE

Brightly
E♭6
N.C.
Girl: With my
Boy: With her
f
mf
E♭6 A♭6/E♭ B♭9 E♭6 A♭6/E♭ B♭9
high starched col - lar and my high - topped shoes and my
high starched col - lar and her high - topped shoes and her
E♭6 B♭9 E♭6 Edim7
hair piled high up - on my head, I
hair piled high up - on her head, she

Fm7 B♭9 E♭ Gm
went to lose a jol - ly hour on the trol - ley and
went to find a jol - ly hour on the trol - ley and
Cm7♭5 F7 Fm7 B♭7
lost my heart in - stead. With his
found my heart in - stead. With my
E♭6 A♭6/E♭ B♭9 E♭6 A♭6/E♭ B♭9
light brown der - by and his bright green tie, he was
light brown der - by and my bright green tie, I was
E♭6 D7 Gm(add9) Gm Cm7♭5
quite the hand - som - est of men. I
quite the lone - som - est of men. I

B♭
F9/B♭
6fr
B♭maj7
F9/B♭
start - ed to yen, so I count - ed to ten, then I
start - ed to yen, so I count - ed to ten, then I
B♭
F9sus
F7
B♭7sus
B♭7
count - ed to ten a - gain.
count - ed to ten a - gain.
gliss. on white keys
E♭6
E♭6
"Clang, clang, clang," went the trol - ley,
"Clang, clang, clang," went the trol - ley,

Fm7/E♭
B♭7/E♭
"Ding, ding, ding," went the bell,
"Ding, ding, ding," went the bell,
E♭7
A♭maj7
A♭m(maj7)
A♭m
"Zing, zing, zing," went my heart - strings, for the
"Zing, zing, zing," went my heart - strings, for the
E♭6
Cm7
Fm7
B♭7
E♭6
mo - ment I saw him I fell.
mo - ment I saw her I fell.
f
dim.
mf
"Chug, chug, chug," went the
"Chug, chug, chug," went the

mo - tor, "Bump, bump, bump," went the
mo - tor, "Bump, bump, bump," went the
Fm7/E♭
B♭7/E♭
6fr
E♭7
brake, "Thump, thump, thump," went my
brake, "Thump, thump, thump," went my
A♭maj7
A♭m(maj7)
4fr
A♭m
4fr
E♭6
Cm7
3fr
Fm7
B♭7
heart - strings, when he smiled, I could feel the car
heart - strings, when she smiled, I could feel the car
E♭6
shake. He tipped his
shake. I tipped my
f
mp

Fm7
Bb7
Eb6
hat, and took a seat. He said he
hat, and took a seat. I said I
Fm7
Bb7
Eb6
hoped he had - n't stepped up - on my feet. He asked my
hoped I had - n't stepped up - on her feet. I asked her
Am7b5
D7
Gm7
Bbm
name, I held my breath. I could - n't
name, then lost my breath. She looked so
F/A
Gm7
C7
F7sus
F7
Fm7/Bb
Bb7b9
speak be - cause he scared me half to death.
love - ly that it scared me half to death.

E♭6
"Buzz, buzz, buzz," went the buzz - er,
"Buzz, buzz, buzz," went the buzz - er,
Fm7/E♭
B♭7/E♭
6fr
"Plop, plop, plop," went the wheels,
"Plop, plop, plop," went the wheels,
E♭9
A♭
4fr
A♭m
4fr
"Stop, stop, stop," went my heart - strings, as he
"Stop, stop, stop," went my heart - strings, as she
1
E♭6
B♭7♭9/E♭
6fr
E♭6
A♭m6
4fr
start - ed to go, then I start - ed to know how it
start - ed to go, then I start - ed to know how it

E♭6/G
G♭dim7
Fm7
B♭9
B♭7♯5
feels when the un - i - verse
feels when the un - i - verse
E♭maj7
E♭6
Fm7
B♭13
B♭7♯5
reels.
reels.
2
E♭6
B♭7♭9/E♭
E♭6
A♭m6
start - ed to leave I took hold of his sleeve with my
start - ed to leave I took hold of her sleeve with my
E♭6/G
G♭dim7
hand. And as if it were
hand. And as if it were

Fm7
B♭7/F
Edim7
planned
planned
he stayed on with me
she stayed on with me
Fm7
B♭7
E♭6/G
A♭6
G7/B
3fr
and it was grand, just to stand with his hand hold - ing
and it was grand, just to stand with her hand hold - ing
Cm(add9)
Cm
Cm(maj7)
Cm7
Fm7
B♭7
8fr
mine,
mine,
to the end of the
to the end of the
f
E♭6
A♭7
4fr
line.
line.
gliss. on white keys
sffz

THE WAY WE WERE

from the Motion Picture THE WAY WE WERE

Words by ALAN and MARILYN BERGMAN
Music by MARVIN HAMLISCH

Slowly
A
Amaj7
Dmaj7
E7
A
Amaj7
mf
Dmaj7
E7
A
C#m7
4fr
Dmaj7
Mem - 'ries light the cor - ners of my
pic - tures of the smiles we left be -
Mem - 'ries may be beau - ti - ful, and
F#m(add2)
F#m/E
Dmaj7
C#m7
4fr
C#7
F#m
F#m/E
To Coda
mind. Mist - y wa - ter - col - or mem - 'ries
hind, smiles we gave to one an - oth - er
yet, what's too pain - ful to re - mem - ber

1
Dmaj7 E7sus E7 Amaj7 F♯m7 Bm7 D/E
of the way we were. Scat-tered
for the way we
2
Amaj7 A7 Dmaj7 C♯m7 4fr Bm7
were. Can it be that it was all so sim-ple then,
C♯m7 4fr F♯7sus F♯7 Bm7 Bm7/A
or has time re-writ-ten ev-'ry line? If we had the chance to do it
E7sus E7 Amaj7 D/E E7
D.S. al Coda
all a-gain, tell me, would we? Could we?

CODA
Dmaj7
C#7sus
C#7
F#m7
F#m/E
Dmaj7
we sim - ply choose to for - get.
So it's the
C#m7
Dmaj7
C#m7
laugh - ter we will re - mem - ber,
Dmaj7
C#m7
F#m7
Bm7
Bm7/E
when - ev - er we re - mem - ber the way we
Amaj7
Dmaj7
D/E
Amaj7
Dmaj7
Amaj7
were; the way we were.
rit.

UP WHERE WE BELONG

from the Paramount Picture AN OFFICER AND A GENTLEMAN

Words by WILL JENNINGS
Music by BUFFY SAINTE-MARIE and JACK NITZSCHE

Em7
A
road is long. There are
D
D/F♯
G
G/B
moun - tains in our way, but we
C
A
G/A
3fr
A
D
D/F♯
climb a
climb them a
step ev - 'ry day. Love, lift us up where we be - long,
cresc.
f
G
Bm
Em
D/F♯
C
G
A
where the ea - gles cry on a moun - tain high.

D D/F♯ G Bm
Love, lift us up where we be - long, far from the
Em D/F♯ F♯/A♯ Bm Gm D G/D A/D
world we know; up where the clear winds blow.
dim.
G/D Gm6/D G/A A F C/E
mp
clear winds blow. Time goes by,
E♭ B♭/D D♭ A♭/C B♭ Fm7/B♭ B♭ E♭
no time to cry, life's you and I, a - live, to - day.

Eb Eb/G Ab Cm
Love, lift us up where we be - long, where the
Fm Eb/G Db Ab Bb Eb Eb/G
ea - gles cry, on a moun - tain high. Love, lift us up where we be - long
Repeat and Fade
Ab Cm Fm Eb/G G/B Cm Abm
far from the world we know; where the clear winds blow.
Optional Ending
Eb Ab/Eb Bb/Eb Ab/Eb Abm6/Eb Eb
8va
rit.
8vb

WHEN SHE LOVED ME

from Walt Disney Pictures' TOY STORY 2 - A Pixar Film

Music and Lyrics by
RANDY NEWMAN

Tenderly, very freely

F/C C7 F B♭
she loved me. Through the sum - mer and the fall, we
F/C Cm/B♭ 8fr F7/A 3fr B♭ F/C B♭ F/C G7/D G7/B C
had each oth - er, that was all. Just she and I to - geth - er, like it was meant to be.
F Gm7 F/A B♭ G7/B Csus2 3fr C F7/A 3fr B♭
And when she was lone - ly, I was there to com - fort her, and I knew that
F/C C7 F
she loved me.

Dm Bbm6/Db F/C G/B Gdim/Bb F/A Fm6/Ab
2fr 6fr
So the years went by; I stayed the same. But she be - gan to drift a - way;
Eb/Bb A7 Dm Bbm6/Db C7 Abm/Cb Bb7
6fr 2fr 4fr
I was left a - lone. Still I wait - ed for the day when she'd say,
Gb6/Db Abm/C C7/E F Gm7 F/A
3fr
"I will al - ways love you." Lone - ly and for - got - ten,
rit.
a tempo
Bb G7/B Csus2 C Em7b5 A/C# Dm F(add2)/C Bb(add2) C
3fr 3fr
nev - er thought she'd look my way, and she smiled at me and held me just like she used to do, like she

F7/A
B♭
F/C
C7sus2
C7
F
Gm7
F/A
3fr
loved me when she loved me. When some - bod - y loved me,
B♭
G7/B
Csus2
C
Em7♭5
A/C♯
Dm
F(add2)/C
ev - 'ry - thing was beau - ti - ful. Ev - 'ry hour we spent to - geth - er
B♭(add2)
C
F/C
C7
lives with - in my heart, when she loved
F
me.

THE WIND BENEATH MY WINGS

from the Original Motion Picture BEACHES

Words and Music by LARRY HENLEY
and JEFF SILBAR

Slowly flowing, in 2
Gmaj7
C
D/C
C
mp
G(add2)
C
D/C
It must have been cold there in my shad - ow,
G(add2)
to nev - er have sun - light on your
C
D/C
C
Am(add2)
face.
You've been con - tent

D7sus
D7
to let me shine,
Am(add2)
D7sus
you al - ways walked the step be - hind.
D7
G(add2)
I was the one with all the
C
D/C
G(add2)
glo - ry,
while you were the one

D/C
C
with all the strength,
Am(add2)
D7sus
on - ly a face
with - out a name,
D7
Am(add2)
I nev - er once
heard you com -
D
B/D♯
4fr
Em
plain.
Did you ev - er know

C G D/F♯ D Em
that you're my he - ro, and ev-'ry - thing
C G D/F♯ C/E D Em
I'd like to be? I can fly high-
C G D/F♯ D Am7
- er than an ea - gle, 'cause you are the wind
To Coda
Am7/D D7 Gmaj9
be - neath my wings.

C
D/C
G(add2)
It might have ap - peared _ to go un-
C
D/C
G(add2)
no - ticed
that I've got it all _
C
D/C
C
_ here in my heart.
Am(add2)
D7sus
I want you to know _ I know the truth:

D7
Am(add2)
I would be noth - in' with - out
D
B/D♯
4fr
D.S. al Coda
you.
CODA
Gmaj9
wings.
C
D/C
Am7/D
D7
You are the wind beneath my
G(add2)
C
D/C
wings.

THE WINDMILLS OF YOUR MIND

from THE THOMAS CROWN AFFAIR

Words by ALAN and MARILYN BERGMAN
Music by MICHEL LEGRAND

Gmaj7
Cmaj7
F♯m7♭5
moon.
stream.
Like a clock whose hands are sweep-ing past the min-utes of its face, And the world is like an
B7
A♯dim7
B7
ap - ple whirl - ing si - lent - ly in space, Like the cir - cles that you find in the wind-mills of your
Em
mind! Keys that jin - gle in your pock - et, words that jan - gle in your
Am7
D7
4fr
head. Why did sum - mer go so quick - ly? Was it some - thing that you

Gmaj7
G7
Cmaj7
said? Lov - ers walk a - long a shore and leave their foot-prints in the sand. Is the sound of dis - tant
F♯7
Bm
drum - ming just the fin - gers of your hand? Pic - tures hang - ing in a
E7
Am
D7
hall - way and the frag - ment of a song. Half re - mem - bered names and fac - es, but to whom do they be -
Gmaj7
Cmaj7
long? When you knew that it was o - ver, you were sud - den - ly a -
(Girl: When you knew that it was o - ver in the au - tumn of good -

F♯m7♭5
4fr
B7
ware That the au - tumn leaves were turn - ing to the col - or of her
byes, For a mo - ment you could not re - call the col - or of his
rit. poco a poco
Em
hair! Like a cir - cle in a spi - ral, like a wheel with - in a
eyes!)
a tempo
B7
A♯dim7
wheel, Nev - er end - ing or be - gin - ning on an ev - er spin - ning reel. As the im - ag - es un -
Em/B
B7
Em
wind, Like the cir - cles that you find in the wind - mills of your mind!
rit. poco a poco

YOU LIGHT UP MY LIFE

from YOU LIGHT UP MY LIFE

Words and Music by
JOSEPH BROOKS

Moderately slow
B♭m
B♭m
E♭
3fr
So man - y nights I'd
Roll - in' at sea, a -
mp
A♭
4fr
Fm
Gm7
C7
sit by my win - dow wait - ing for some - one to
drift on the wa - ters, could it be fi - n'lly I'm
Fm
F7
B♭m
E♭
3fr
sing me his song. So man - y dreams I
turn - ing for home? Fi - n'lly a chance to

A♭ A♭/G Fm G
kept deep in - side me, a - lone in the dark, but now
say, "Hey! I love you." Nev - er a - gain to
B♭7 Fm7 B♭7 E♭
you've come a - long.
be all a - lone.
And you
mf
E♭maj7 E♭7
light up my life. You give me
C7 Fm
hope to car - ry on. You

Fm7
B♭7
To Coda
light up my days and fill my
1
E♭
B♭/D
Cm
Fm
B♭7
3fr
nights with song.
2
E♭
B♭/D
Cm
Fm
nights with song.
B♭
D.S. al Coda
'Cause
CODA
G
nights with

Cm
3fr
F
E♭
3fr
song.
It can't be wrong ___ when
G
Cm
3fr
F
it feels so right, ___ 'cause
E♭/B♭
6fr
E♭sus/B♭
6fr
B♭
A♭
4fr
E♭
3fr
B♭
you, ___ you light up my ___
A♭
4fr
E♭
3fr
life. ___
rit.

YOU'VE GOT A FRIEND IN ME

from Walt Disney's TOY STORY

Music and Lyrics by
RANDY NEWMAN

A♭ E♭/G G7 Cm
and miles from your nice warm bed,
There is - n't an - y - thing I would - n't do for you.
A♭ D/A E♭/B♭ G/B Cm A♭7 G Cm
you just re - mem - ber what your old pal said: Son, you've
If we stick to - geth - er we can see it through, 'cause you've
F7 B♭7 E♭ C7 F7 B♭7
got a friend in me. Yeah, you've got a friend in me.
got a friend in me. Yeah, you've got a friend in me.
1
E♭ G7/D Cm B7 E♭/B♭ E♭dim/B♭ B♭7

2
E♭ E♭maj7 E♭7 A♭ D
Now, some oth - er folks might be a lit - tle bit smart - er than I am,
E♭6 D7 E♭6 D Em7
big - ger and strong - er, too. May - be. But none of them will
Fdim7 D/F♯ Gm C7 Fm B♭7
ev - er love you the way I do, just me and you, boy.
E♭ B♭7♯5 E♭7 A♭ Adim7
And as the years go by, our friend - ship will nev - er die.

E♭/B♭
E♭
A♭
Adim7
E♭/B♭
G7/B
Cm
You're gon - na see it's our des - ti - ny.
molto rit.
F7
B♭7
E♭
C7
F7
B♭7
You've got a friend in me.
You've got a friend in me.
a tempo
E♭
C7
F7
B♭7
E♭
G7/D
You've got a friend in me.
Cm
B7
E♭/B♭
E♭dim/B♭
B♭7
E♭
rit.

WHEN YOU WISH UPON A STAR

from Walt Disney's PINOCCHIO

Words by NED WASHINGTON
Music by LEIGH HARLINE

Cdim C C6/G C/E E♭dim7 Dm Am/E F F/G G9 G7♭9
3fr
9fr
who you are, an - y - thing your heart de - sires will come to
Cmaj7 G13 G7 C A7 Dm Dm7 G7
3fr
you. If your heart is in your dream, no re - quest is
Cdim C C6/G C/E E♭dim7 Dm Am/E F F/G G9
3fr
9fr
too ex - treme, when you wish up - on a star as dream - ers
C Fm6/G Em/G Cmaj7 C6 Dm/G Gdim G7
do. Fate is kind, she brings to

Cdim C Am D7
those who love, the sweet ful - fill - ment of their se - cret
Fm6 G7 G7♯5(♭9) G7 C A7 Dm Dm7
long - ing. Like a bolt out of the blue,
G7 Cdim C C6/G C/E E♭dim7 Dm Am/E F
fate steps in and sees you thru, when you wish up - on a star your
1 F/G G9 G7♭9 C G13 G7
dream comes true.
2 F/G G7 C
dream comes true.